SCHOOLS FOR THE FUTURE

Designs for Learning Communities

ding Bulletin 95

Londo

The Stationery Office

'Inside and outside the design
is different from any other
school. It looks like an office
– it is a working environment.'

'I am proud of the school.'

'The facilities are
great. I like the
whiteboards and PCs.'

'The organisation is really great. All exits are easy
to get to. You can get from one place to another
with the minimum of fuss.'

'The library is beautiful –
the spiral staircase and
the windows make it a
peaceful place to work.'

'The design of the school
is really important.'

Children's responses to their new school, The Lammas School, Leyton.

INTRODUCTION

Education has a vital role to play in creating a fair and a just society, building strong communities and developing a knowledge based economy. Education is the route to equality of opportunity for all and can help people to release their potential not only during their time at school but also throughout their working lives.

The recent White Paper, Schools – Achieving Success, highlighted the drive to focus more closely than ever before on the needs, aptitudes and aspirations of individual pupils. As changing social and economic conditions increase the need for learning, so too technological advances alter the way that we learn. The White Paper sets out a major agenda for transforming secondary education in particular, with greater institutional diversity combined with new ways of helping schools work with one another. Key developments for the future that are reflected in the document include:

- Increased use of information and communication technology (ICT), across the curriculum and age range;
- Greater flexibility in the curriculum;
- An emphasis on 'early years' provision, both alongside schools and as part of cross-sector centres;
- Inclusion of more pupils with special educational needs in mainstream schools;
- 'Opening up' of the school to a range of users;
- An increase in the number of school support staff.

Government expenditure on capital works at schools is set to increase sharply over the next few years giving Local Education Authorities (LEAs) and schools greater opportunities to improve their school buildings. It is essential that funds are spent wisely and a range of funding sources are investigated – both public and private – across the Authority as a whole. This is particularly relevant as schools become focal points for their communities, providing a range of family and community services. New school or refurbishment projects that are undertaken will also need to address the major initiatives in the construction industry including:

- The promotion of good design in public buildings, along the lines encouraged by the Commission for Architecture and the Built Environment (CABE);
- The development of designs which will minimise the environmental impact of building through various means such as low energy use;
- Working to achieve the targets of Rethinking Construction, like reduced wastage, improved delivery time and better value for money.

This publication touches on all these issues and considers their accommodation implications. Its intention is to inspire good quality design that serves the needs of pupils and the wider community. Part 1 looks in detail at the changes in education and government priorities. Part 2 examines the design implications for these developments while Part 3 considers how to achieve design quality and value for money in the building process. The advice is applicable to the adaptation of existing buildings as well as new building projects. It is intended for everyone involved with school design including local authority officers, consultants and promoters as well as headteachers and school governors. More information and an electronic version of this guidance can be found at www.teachernet.gov.uk/schoolbuildings.

Left to right: Alfred Salter School, Southwark, London; Park Grove Primary School, York. Opposite page: Royal Docks School, Newham, London.

KEY ISSUES FOR THE 21ST CENTURY SCHOOL

Education is a recognised priority, not just for the Government, but also for society as a whole. It is the key to preparing the nation for the emergence of the knowledge economy and its increased demands for skills and human capital.

Despite their importance to successful education, many school buildings are of poor design, are dull and uniform and have an institutional look. To succeed in raising educational standards and improving attainment levels we need to examine how to make our existing schools better and ensure that new school buildings are well designed and built.

If schools are to provide excellent educational facilities for the next 20 to 30 years, designs for new school buildings and major adaptations need to take account of current and likely future developments in education and technology. Schools, LEAs and designers need to be aware of key drivers for change in schools, including the likely impact of a more diverse curriculum; new ways of learning and the impact of ICT; opening up the school to other pupils and the community as a whole and the inclusion of pupils with special educational needs into mainstream schools.

As new school buildings will serve their communities for many years to come it is important that they are high quality, attractive buildings. Design quality encompasses a number of issues but should include sustainability, flexibility and adaptability, and value for money.

Part 1 outlines the issues mentioned above which all need to be considered when briefing for and designing school buildings to ensure that they are fit for their purpose and enjoyable to use. The sections are as follows:

1.1   Schools and the changing curriculum
1.2   New ways of learning and the impact of ICT
1.3   Blurring the school boundaries
1.4   Inclusion
1.5   Design quality and sustainability

SOHAM VILLAGE COLLEGE, ELY, CAMBRIDGESHIRE
This technology college accommodates 1300 11 to 16 year olds and shares its site with a training centre for local businesses. Technology is a prominent part of the curriculum and in 1999 pupils took part in a project to build this hovercraft which actually 'flies'. The school has also set up an on-line learning system.

1.1 SCHOOLS AND THE CHANGING CURRICULUM

The school curriculum is becoming broader and more flexible. While the National Curriculum remains as a framework, schools are being encouraged to offer a diverse range of provision to suit local circumstances, often in partnership with the local community, including business. Schools are being encouraged to develop more flexible curriculum pathways, particularly from the age of 14, to provide an education that matches the talents and aspirations of individuals.

There are already specialist secondary schools which have developed centres of excellence in particular areas of the curriculum such as music and the arts, sports, modern experience and enterprise initiatives, and to develop links with business. From September 2002, vocational GCSEs will be introduced, encouraging more pupils to combine vocational and general study.

Modern apprenticeships in skilled occupations will become increasingly commonplace. Qualifications that count towards apprenticeships could be gained while pupils are still at school. Work experience may be arranged with local businesses which also offer apprenticeship places. There will be scope for increasing the time available for vocational study within the statutory framework of the National Curriculum, in particular work-based

> **'Building the curriculum – particularly beyond the age of 14, when the talents of pupils diversify – around the needs of each individual, with far better opportunities for vocational and academic study.'**
>
> Schools - Achieving Success (DfES White Paper), 2001

languages and science. Schools with specialist facilities are often regional centres whose specialist facilities are available to other schools and the community as a whole. Electronic access to skilled teachers can enable the study of minority subjects such as Latin or Japanese.

There are also increased possibilities for vocational options. 14-18 year old pupils are being encouraged to undertake independent research and study, taking part in a range of work-related activities, such as work

There are increased possibilities for vocational options.

PERTHCELYN COMMUNITY PRIMARY SCHOOL, SOUTH WALES
Community and school can work together on the curriculum.

The National Curriculum remains as a framework for education with literacy and numeracy hours being a key part of its delivery.

study for craft and vocational learning, progressing to an apprenticeship option.

There are also changes to the post-16 curriculum taking place. These are partly in response to dissatisfaction with A-level courses. Some students see them as the path of least resistance towards getting a job; other pupils don't even stay on post-16, many of them feeling that elements of the curriculum are no longer relevant. Other contributory factors include pupils feeling a lack of recognition for their work and a lack of good social areas for pupils. (See Section 2A.5 on social and movement spaces).

Schools and colleges are now able to offer young people opportunities to study a more diverse range of subjects post-16. These include AS qualifications, designed to encourage the take-up of a wider range of subjects in the first year of post-16 study, and vocational A-levels replacing advanced GNVQs.

In September 2000, the government introduced a new stage of education for three to five year olds: the foundation stage. Early learning goals were established to improve continuity between early years education and primary schooling. It is accepted that children will be learning in a range of places at this age, including nursery schools and at home with a childminder. Specially designated Early Excellence Centres reflect best practice in early years education.

These curriculum developments and qualification changes are likely to affect the character of schools and their accommodation requirements.

KINGSMEAD PRIMARY SCHOOL, ENTRY INTO RIBA SUSTAINABLE SCHOOLS COMPETITION
The new foundation stage should improve educational continuity for three to five year old children.

BURTON BOROUGH SCHOOL, SHROPSHIRE
Vocational options range from the performing arts, a specialism in this school, to catering.

PARK GROVE PRIMARY SCHOOL, YORK
Schools should offer a variety of learning experiences and incorporate the best in modern technology.

Multi-media equipment is particularly valuable for teaching and studying subjects such as modern foreign languages, helping to set the languages in context.

1.2 NEW WAYS OF LEARNING AND THE IMPACT OF ICT

The ways in which people learn are changing. These changes are being driven partly by the need for different skills for new ways of living and working, and partly by a concern that people are not reaching their full potential. Learning is also being affected by the extensive use of information and communications technology (ICT).

New ways of learning

Education must change to enable us to cope with changes in society. For example, employment in one steady career throughout a lifetime is now rare and many people need to be able to work around the world as business and culture generally becomes more international. The qualities that are essential to meet these challenges are:

- Adaptability to suit changing technology and allow mobility;
- Willingness and ability to work in dynamic teams;
- Passion for learning throughout life;
- Creativity (public and private institutions are changing rapidly as a result of economic and cultural demands and a creative workforce is required to manage these changes);
- Ability to organise and analyse information.

If pupils are to have a stimulating learning experience which leads them to acquire these skills, some change in the methods of learning is likely. Successful methods include:

- Active learning, individually or in a group,

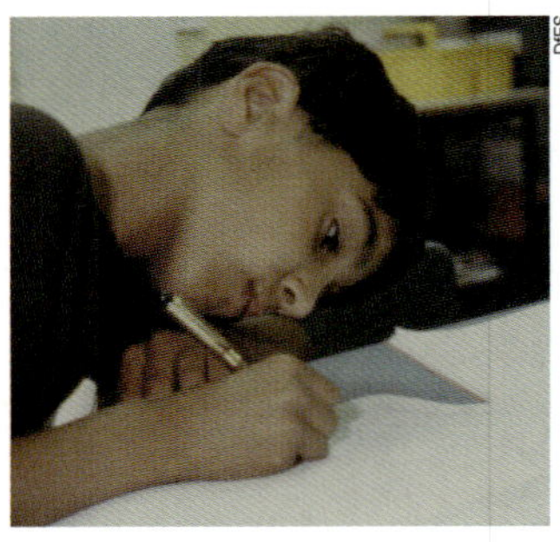

A willingness to learn new things, and adapt creatively throughout life is vital to meeting the future challenges of society.

ARBOUR VALE, SLOUGH
Over the last three years, Arbour Vale School has been developing video-conferencing as a learning tool. An international directory of schools and other establishments that are willing to provide lectures or take part in discussion groups has enabled Arbour Vale and neighbouring schools to 'talk' to schools in France and Italy, as well as listen to experts talking from Athens, California and Japan. The school feels that SEN pupils in particular respond well to the interactive style and the 'reality' of the experience.

WILLOWTREE PRIMARY SCHOOL, EALING, LONDON
This new school was designed to be technology rich. All classrooms have electronic whiteboards and pupils can use computers in the shared activity area and in separate ICT spaces. Staff have ICT access and make good use of e-mail which has vastly reduced the amount of paperwork.

FRENSHAM HEIGHTS SCHOOL, HAMPSHIRE
Working informally with other pupils can be a valuable learning experience - a variety of experience is the key to stimulating learning. The practice of working with dynamic teams can help prepare young people for our changing society and employment culture.

FOREST GATE CITY LEARNING CENTRE, NEWHAM, LONDON
Facilities at this City Learning Centre are shared between neighbouring schools and the local community.

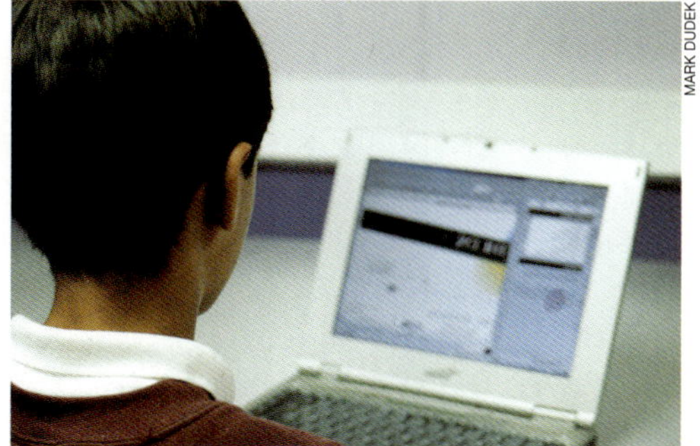

With ICT, individualised work plans can be devised for pupils, allowing them to learn at their own pace. In the future, pupils may have their own hardware.

Video link-ups can reduce isolation, particularly for those with special needs.

including information-gathering as well as practical experiences such as doing scientific experiments;

- Learning in a context, drawing a number of ideas together by common themes (a way of learning currently familiar at primary level);
- Learning at the individual's own pace, which is often difficult to achieve if all learning is gained through lecture-style teaching;
- Variety in the learning experience, whether different teachers, different co-learners, different places or different styles of learning.

Working individually allows learners to set their own pace on projects that place their learning in context. However, individual work should not totally supplant other experiences (for example, an over-emphasis on computers for individual learning can lead to isolation). Group working develops social awareness and builds team working skills. It is also a valuable means of presenting ideas; it is a key part, for example, in primary literacy and numeracy hours. One important result of more independent working is that it tends to lead to higher adult/pupil ratios because guidance is needed, although a lighter 'collegiate' touch can be effective. Adults can include parents or others with specialist knowledge, business partners or support staff.

ICT and the way we learn

Developments in ICT have had, and will continue to have, a profound effect on teaching and learning. Computers are now an essential tool for learning. The number of computers in schools will continue to increase and, in the future, it is likely that all pupils will have their own (wireless) hardware. Electronic whiteboards, scanners and colour printers are also becoming valuable teaching aids. Where practical activities are prohibitively expensive or even dangerous, technology now allows pupils to have 'virtual' practical experience. Good quality recordings of speech and music mean that oral skills can be learnt and assessed more easily.

Government initiatives are supporting the use of new technologies through the National Grid for Learning programme for funding infrastructure and connectivity; the NOF teacher training programme; initiatives such as Curriculum Online; and developments such as City Learning Centres which are being established to support a number of schools.

Used imaginatively, ICT can open up new learning opportunities. It should be seen as a creative tool that encourages learners to be actively involved in learning, enabling creativity and helping people to develop their learning and thinking skills. It can give access to an enormous amount of information (hence our need to learn how to handle and critique information), which can be accessed and contributed to from anywhere at any time. Pupils can learn from, and with, others across the network – whether using the internet or video link-ups – reducing isolation for outlying schools. They can communicate their ideas around the world, which is important to young people today who expect the right to be heard.

ICT contributes to inclusion by offering multiple media opportunities that may engage some students previously alienated from education. In different contexts, and with different students, video, sound, speech, graphics and different cultural representations can close the 'inclusion gap' dramatically.

ICT helps teachers to create personalised work plans to encourage individualised learning, making it easier for pupils of different ages and abilities to work more easily together. Students can be continuously assessed from a distance and records of achievement can be kept for a lifetime in a 'digital vault'. ICT can also enable remote access to school networks by teachers, which could help to improve their work/life balance by allowing greater flexibility in working time and place.

These new ways of learning, including increasing use of ICT, will have an effect on the balance of spaces in a school of the future.

ALLFARTHING SCHOOL, WANDSWORTH, LONDON
Allfarthing is at the leading edge of primary school technology and is part of a scheme which aims to give the children, staff and wider community better skills in ICT. The school has taken part in the BBC's Web Wise Campaign, allowing people from the community to come in and experience using the internet, maybe for the first time. The school has started running a cybercafé which parents can visit and pay to have access to the internet for an hour. The school also has three digital cameras and several scanners which Key Stage 2 children use for multi-media learning.

CREATIVE PARTNERSHIPS PROGRAMME
This cooperative programme enables children to develop skills and creativity by bringing schools together with theatres, galleries and other providers of the arts and create sustainable partnerships with on-going visits and activities. The Sporting Future for All Initiative links schools to local sports clubs while the current Museums and Galleries Programme supports over 60 projects aimed at developing educational links between schools and museums and galleries. Here children are examining a dinosaur skeleton at the Natural History Museum in London.

1.3 BLURRING THE SCHOOL BOUNDARIES

While the school is likely to continue to be the key learning base for 3 to 16/18 year olds in the future, the boundaries between school and the outside world will be less clearly defined. The government is encouraging schools to open up their buildings to a range of other users during the school day and beyond. At the same time, there are more opportunities for pupils to learn outside school and beyond the school day. Learning is going beyond formal education, becoming a lifelong process, helping people to maximise their potential throughout their working and family lives.

Opening up the school
Following a commitment given in the White Paper, Schools – Achieving Success, the Government is encouraging schools to develop as focal points for a range of family and community services. A new legal power is being introduced to make it easier for governors to provide these wider services. The range provided will differ from one school to another and depend on local need, but might include childcare, health and social services, adult and family learning, recreational facilities, ICT access, and possibly legal or housing advice.

The experiences of Sure Start and Early Excellence Centres have shown that the needs of children and their families are best met by easily accessible, joined-up services. Provision of on-site health, social and other support can help to improve educational standards by addressing the range of needs of pupils and

GRANDVIEW UUQINAK'UH COMMUNITY SCHOOLYARD, CANADA
Schools can be the focal point for family and community services. This school has a community garden and an outdoor meeting room that groups can use.

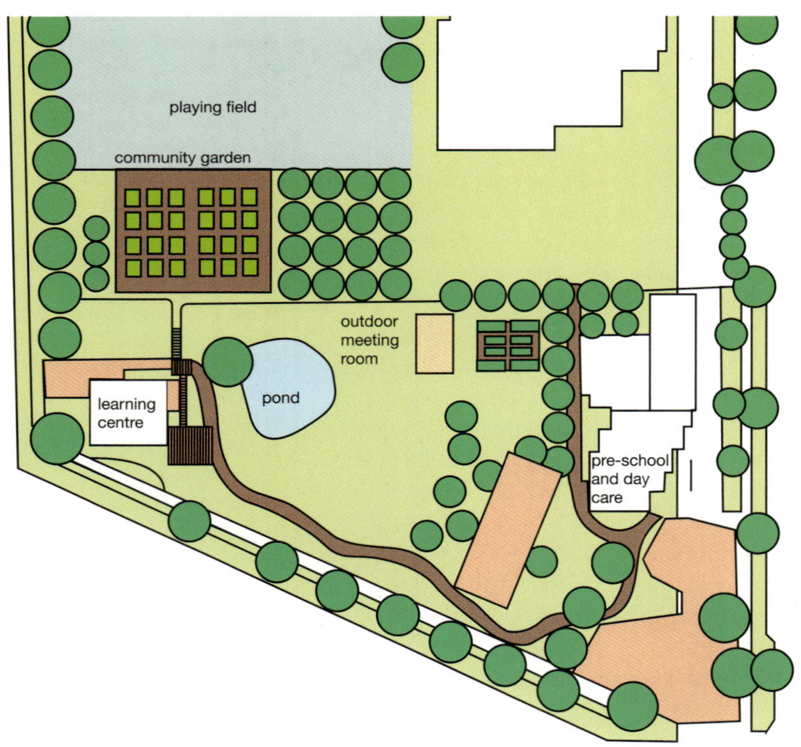

An on-site crèche can benefit school staff and adults attending courses on the site.

Many schools already share their hall with the community. In the future most schools are likely to open up the school for a large part of the day, throughout the year.

THE ACE CENTRE, CENTRE OF EXCELLENCE FOR EARLY YEARS, OXFORDSHIRE
This centre provides community learning and support at a variety of levels, including keep fit classes, IT training and support for adults with learning difficulties. A hall and classroom are available for adult use throughout the day and evening.

their families which prevent children from reaching their full potential. For instance, underlying pupil health and motivation problems can be more easily dealt with by on-site medical, mental health, counselling and social services, with minimal disruption to children's learning. Provision of childcare and recreational facilities can ensure children have safe and stimulating opportunities to play and learn, and can relieve pressure on families.

Where schools have started to develop these wider services, parents tend to become more involved in the school and therefore more supportive of their children's learning. Research has shown that parental involvement is one of the key factors in a pupil's performance (Dyson and Robson, 1999). Adult and family learning in particular can help raise adults' expectations of their children, while they themselves may be encouraged to continue their own education at a higher level.

Schools developing in this way can help to bring together different community groups, and in deprived communities can make a key contribution to neighbourhood renewal. Training and ICT facilities provided by the school can help meet local employment needs and enable people to keep pace with changing technology. Co-location of services can be particularly valuable in rural areas, where services are currently often spread out over a wide area, making them difficult to access.

Teachers and school staff will also benefit from being able to easily access services such as healthcare and childcare during their working day.

Schools in the future will therefore embrace a wide range of users including:

MILLENNIUM PRIMARY SCHOOL, GREENWICH, LONDON
Built in 2001, the Millennium Primary School and Health Centre, set within the pioneering Millennium Village, is a community facility providing education and healthcare on one site. The primary school is for 420 5-11 year olds. There is also an early years centre (EYC) for one to four year olds and a crèche for the use of parents attending the health centre or activities in the school. The EYC offers an extended day to under-fives for 48 weeks of the year, and the main school houses holiday play schemes. To further extend the school day the school's food technology space has a sitting and eating area for breakfast, afternoon snacks and socialising, before and after school. The school and EYC are fully inclusive of children with SEN. Physiotherapy and other services are available in the health centre, and specialists come to the school to work with pupils.

The health centre alongside the school provides a full range of primary care as well as promoting healthy living and preventative approaches to medicine. Its reception area includes a one-stop shop for information and advice. The centre supplies some specialist services to pupils with SEN, and in turn shares use of the crèche, and SEN and community spaces in the school for meetings, exercise classes or courses.

The school itself has been designed for community use offering a wide range of adult education classes and training during the school day. Parts of the school are also available out of hours. To cope with visitors, the reception area is bigger than usual and designed for separate access by – and security for – the different user groups. The hall is big enough for recreational badminton or other indoor games and is equipped for theatrical events and suitable for religious use. The school playground is also easily accessible out-of-hours.

BOURNEMOUTH CLASSROOM OF THE FUTURE PROJECT
The proposal is to establish an out-of-school learning centre with links to schools in the area and beyond. The project involves three sites: a hub and two satellites. The hub will be located at a Site of Special Scientific Interest, allowing the opportunity to explore seven distinct local habitats, a variety of conservation issues and the area's Stone Age and Iron Age archaeological inheritance. The satellites will be constructed at two schools which have been prioritised for increased accommodation and there will be electronic links to all secondary schools in the South West Grid for Learning. Advanced technology connecting to remote centres from the Scottish glens to the Galapagos Islands, will include stereoscopic cameras, enabling students to conduct and record field studies remotely in three dimensions.

TEACHING METHODS

A recent study commissioned by the DfEE examined various methods of teaching in secondary schools. Types under the microscope included team teaching, partial withdrawal and support teaching. The study found that greater flexibility and choice was welcomed by pupils and parents. It also suggested that a longer school day could increase timetable flexibility.

- Pre-school children — for childcare, playgroup or crèche;
- Parents involved in school life or attending family related courses;
- Adults (including parents) and children using school facilities for educational, and recreational purposes, and to access services such as health care;
- Adults giving support to pupils through classroom support or mentoring;
- Local employers using school facilities for training.

Arrangements for sharing the school's accommodation will vary greatly depending on such factors as location, school size and age range. Good transport links and appropriate accommodation will also be important. While some schools may not at present feel able to open up to the community during the school day, most schools in the future are likely to have at least some facilities open to the whole community from early morning to late evening, throughout the year. DfEE guidance Raising Standards: Opening Doors has useful advice on community use. DfES will be publishing further guidance on how to develop community services in schools, to accompany the new legislation.

Increased breadth and flexibility

A pupil's learning experience is going to be less and less restricted to their school base and the traditional school timetable. Many pupils are already studying before and after school, at lunch times, weekends and during the summer holidays (for example at homework clubs or courses for gifted and talented children). Pupils are also going beyond the school to other learning centres such as museums and galleries, or gaining real workplace experience. In the future there is likely to be greater movement between schools as each school is encouraged to develop a speciality. This increase in diversity combined with increased collaboration is a key part of the recent White Paper, Schools — Achieving Success:

'The diverse system we want to build will be one where schools differ markedly from each other in the particular contribution they choose to

CHAFFORD HUNDRED LEARNING CAMPUS, THURROCK, ESSEX
This is an all age (3-16) community school with places for 210 primary pupils (plus a 26-place nursery) and 600 secondary pupils. A team made up of two heads and personnel from the local adult college and Thurrock library service manage the campus. To encourage everyday co-operation there is a joint heads' room and a joint staffroom. Having an all-age school allows older primary pupils to use science laboratories, music rooms and have some access to better PE facilities. The community has access to recreation facilities, library and all secondary spaces during the day and PE spaces outside school hours. An on-site crèche allows parents to attend classes.

make but where all are equally excellent in giving their students a broad curriculum and the opportunity to achieve high standards. Far from concentrating success in a few schools, diversity is about motivating individual schools, spreading excellence, sharing success and working collaboratively.'

A change of place can help stimulate learning. Of course not all movement has to be physical, as technology allows electronic links to be made to other places.

Some schools are exploring alternatives to the traditional timetable and this is likely to increase in the future. A more flexible school day with more freedom for pupils to choose when they take breaks or eat lunch could allow pupils to study in their free time, after school or at home. This arrangement, with similarities to higher education or office work patterns, may be more applicable at secondary than primary level. The accommodation implications of these new ways of learning are discussed in Part 2.

Variations in the organisational structure of schools are also emerging. All-age campuses are being considered as part of an attempt to make the learning sequence more seamless. Mixed-age teaching is possible, with older pupils helping younger ones, so reducing problems associated with the transition from primary to middle and secondary schools.

School structures are being freed by ICT. Small rural schools, for example, can form federations which are linked electronically. This allows teachers with specialist knowledge to reach a wider audience and pupils in mixed age groups to work with their peers at a distance. Pupils who have difficulty attending school at all can learn from somewhere else such as their home rather than missing valuable learning time.

BA WATERSIDE CENTRE, HILLINGDON, LONDON
The Learning Centre was set up two years ago as part of British Airways' community relations programme. It provides an alternative learning experience for local schools, has links with colleges and universities and is open for family courses out of school hours. Most teaching takes place at the centre but staff also visit schools. The centre has developed a particular interest in sustainability and the environment, making use of its large area of parkland. Courses are not static, however, and are developed with schools to meet their curriculum needs. Much of the layout is open plan and staff are keen to make it different from a school environment. Areas include an airport waiting area with soft seating, an aeroplane interior and an 'underwater' scene. More traditional teaching areas have round tables and 'non-school' chairs which create an informal and 'adult' atmosphere.

BRIGHTON HILL, BASINGSTOKE, HAMPSHIRE
This 1200-pupil 11-16 secondary school is very full, so from September 2002 the school day will be extended (8.15 to 5.30) to make more effective use of available accommodation, and leaving and arrival times will be staggered. KS3 will arrive first, and finish just after 1pm, when they can either go home or stay for extra-curricular activities. The teaching organisation at KS4 will be flexible, like at a college. Pupils will arrive at 8.30 and stay until 5.30pm, during that time they will have some timetabled time and some supervised private study. KS4 pupils doing GNVQs (longer sessions) can make use of the longer day by taking other options after 4 pm. The school hopes to give pupils the option to work at home by providing them with laptops by 2005.

DUNBURY CHURCH OF ENGLAND VC FIRST SCHOOL, BLANDFORD FORUM, DORSET
Four rural village schools (each with around 50 places, for children between 4 and 9 years old) are arranged in a federation with one head. Each school has two mixed-age classrooms. Schools are networked and use e-mail and video-conferencing to work across the schools. Same-age pupils can send messages to classmates in other schools for joint project work. Video-conferencing may take place one-to-one or as a whole class. There is no special room for this but pupils learn to be quiet when it is taking place. Computers have large screens so that a group can see the screen. The schools also make use of distance learning by linking up with cultural institutions, like the Science Museum. They have also performed joint music and drama projects electronically.

POKESDOWN PRIMARY SCHOOL, BOURNEMOUTH
Physical accessibility throughout the school can assist with inclusion, as with ramps in this school.

Increasing pupil support, whether educational, social or medical, is a key plank of inclusion.

'Where all children are included as equal partners in the school community, the benefits are felt by all.'

Secretary of State, Excellence for all Children (1997)

> **FIRTH PARK COMMUNITY COLLEGE, SHEFFIELD**
> Firth Park Community College is a mixed comprehensive school with 1300 pupils on roll. The school provides pupil support in three main areas: a mentoring system; support for those with SEN and support for those with emotional and behavioural difficulties. There is inevitably a good deal of overlap and co-ordination between these three functions. The four learning mentors, who have varying professional backgrounds, share an office base but also book offices or support rooms around the school for individual sessions with year 10 and 11 students.

1.4 INCLUSION

The Government is committed to promoting inclusion of pupils with Special Educational Needs (SEN) and disabilities into mainstream schools as part of a wider range of policies that recognise and celebrate human diversity. The Special Educational Needs and Disability Act (2001) strengthens the rights of pupils with Special Educational Needs to be educated in mainstream schools. It places new duties on providers to make reasonable adjustments so that disabled pupils are not at a significant disadvantage. There is also a duty to plan for increased accessibility to schools' premises.

Inclusion has a number of meanings all of which have an impact on the school fabric:

- Education within mainstream schools of an increasing number of children with disabilities;
- A broad mix of children – in terms of ability, needs, background, etc – in a single school;
- Participation of children in the full range of opportunities provided by a school, including access to the full curriculum and involvement with social and community activities.

The green paper Excellence for all Children (1997) proposed that as many pupils as possible should be educated in mainstream schools.

There are many overlaps between the increased community use of schools and increased inclusion. 'Inclusion' refers principally to a wide range of learners attending the school full time and 'community' refers to other, part-time users.

One of the key effects of greater inclusion is an increase in pupil support, whether educational, social or medical. The number of para-professionals working in schools has grown considerably in recent years. Outside agencies are also bringing other professionals, such as educational psychologists or social workers, into schools. Schools are also working more closely with parents, encouraging them into schools for meetings and general support. Where there are linked facilities on site, such as health and social care, children with special educational needs and their families can benefit.

All pupils need good pastoral support if they are to succeed in their education and also feel part of the school community. There have been a number of initiatives that aim to improve opportunities for pupils who are not reaching their potential. Arrangements such as mentoring, counselling and house systems can not only help pupils feel more positive about their school experience but also reduce behavioural problems.

1.5 DESIGN QUALITY AND SUSTAINABILITY

There are many examples of well-designed schools. But there is a feeling that the standard of design in public buildings generally has been lower than it should be. In the publication, Better Public Buildings, the Government spelt out its commitment to good design.

Buildings have the power to bring about a change in social behaviour, leading in turn to changes in attitude. A well-designed school can serve its users well and draw a more positive attitude from parents and the wider community. This is particularly relevant to inclusion.

A DfEE study in 1999 which looked at the impact of capital investment on pupil performance showed clear evidence that improvements raised morale of both staff and pupils and assisted with staff retention (Building Performance. An empirical assessment of the relationship between schools capital investment and pupil performance, carried out by PricewaterhouseCoopers for the DfEE).

The Commission for Architecture and the Built Environment (CABE) was set up by the

environment, in terms of energy and water use, materials, waste, transport, site ecology, health and safety and internal environmental conditions. Schools of the future must be designed to avoid wasted investment through early and rapid obsolescence. They need to have a long functional life, demonstrating good value for money in terms of life cycle costs.

The issues of buildability and efficiency were addressed in the 'Rethinking Construction' report of 1998. The report recommended, amongst other things, that the building process should aim to:

- Better meet the needs and expectations of the building's users;
- Achieve targets for reductions in cost, time and defects;
- Create less confrontational working arrangements between client, contractor and consultants.

These issues are discussed further in Part 3 of this document.

KINGSMEAD PRIMARY SCHOOL, CANTERBURY, RIBA SUSTAINABLE SCHOOLS COMPETION ENTRY
The three joint winners of the Royal Institute of British Architects' sustainable schools competition combined good quality design and sustainability.

John Pardey and Sir Colin Stansfield Smith's entry uses the sustainable resource of timber and modular construction to reduce waste. Natural light from clerestory glazing, and stack effect ventilation reduces energy use. A wood chip boiler to provide heating should minimise carbon emissions. Their 'walled garden' design encloses the school and provides a safe haven for children.

> **'I am determined that good design should not be confined to high profile buildings in the big cities; all of the users of public services, wherever they are, should be able to benefit from better design.'**
>
> Rt Hon Tony Blair MP, Prime Minister, Better Public Buildings (2000)

Government in 1999 to help improve the quality of design being delivered through new buildings and spaces. It runs a range of programmes that provide assistance to clients and comment on designs. Good design is more than a beautiful facade, and involves the layout of the building and outside areas, as well as the use of materials and choice of services and fittings. It does not necessarily cost more.

Design quality has been defined as a combination of:

- Functionality;
- Sustainability;
- Buildability;
- Efficiency;
- Aesthetics;
- Durability.

All these apply as much to schools as other building types. They are key to achieving better value for money for all concerned. One of these issues – sustainability – is particularly important at a time when there is growing awareness of environmental responsibility.

The aim of sustainable construction is for buildings to have a low impact on the

WHITELEY PRIMARY SCHOOL, FAREHAM, HAMPSHIRE
This 630-place primary school was built in two phases on a wooded site in Hampshire. The original part of the school, for 420 pupils, consists of a sweep of classrooms facing south onto the woodland, with resource areas, cloakrooms and toilets behind. The main entrance, administration spaces and the hall are centrally positioned on the north side. Consideration has been given to function, sustainability and visual enjoyment. All classrooms are naturally lit and ventilated with direct access to a deck for outside learning. They have views to the south and daylight reaches the backs of classrooms through rooflights. The external areas have been designed as part of the whole with a woodland walk allowing pupils to benefit from their beautiful natural location.

Left to right: Haute Vallee School, Jersey; Charter School, Southwark, London. Opposite page: Glastonbury Thorn Primary School, Buckinghamshire.

2 DESIGN ISSUES FOR SCHOOLS

Schools will remain at the heart of the learning process for children and adults, for the foreseeable future at least. Although ICT allows pupils, in theory, to learn from anywhere at any time, they still need the support of a regular base and a strong community. However, the boundaries between schools and other learning places will be less clear cut and the school of the future will become a resource for the whole community.

There isn't a design blueprint for a school of the future; a variety of models will emerge. The main design challenge facing LEAs and schools is to balance the needs of different users, creating inspiring buildings with functional spaces that are appropriate for new educational developments and new technologies but adaptable enough to cater for the changing needs of the future.

Part 2 looks at the key design issues to be considered when designing a school for today and the future. The guidance applies to both new schools and adaptations at existing schools. Schools can use the guidance for developing long term plans for improving their buildings. Much of the guidance in Part 2 is covered in greater detail in other publications, which are referred to at appropriate parts of the text or hyperlinks provided for the web-based version of the guidance (see www.teachernet.gov.uk/schoolbuildings). The need for a good standard of design is implicit in all recommendations. Part 2 is divided into the following sections:

2A   Spaces for today and tomorrow
2B   The learning environment
2C   Thoughtful planning
2D   Sustainability

EXIT
EXIT

**SUMMERFIELDS NURSERY,
WILMSLOW, MACCLESFIELD**

2A SPACES FOR TODAY AND TOMORROW

This section looks at the range of spaces needed to accommodate the developments outlined in Part I. It considers the effect of the new learning methods (such as more individual working), the changing use of ICT, and the needs of a wider range of users. Size and overall floor area are discussed in principle, but for detailed guidance on gross area and the size of individual spaces see Building Bulletin 82.

The main part of the section looks at all types of school space, whether learning or non-learning, internal or external. The spaces are divided into the following broad groupings for primary and secondary schools:

2A.1   Group spaces
2A.2   Large spaces
2A.3   Resource spaces
2A.4   Support spaces
2A.5   Social and movement
2A.6   Staff areas
2A.7   Service spaces
2A.8   Other services
2A.9   External areas

The introduction looks at two overarching issues: the importance of flexibility and the likely changes to the overall area and balance of spaces required for education in the future.

Flexibility

- A wider range of users and more individual working requires greater flexibility.
- Some ways of achieving flexibility can be costly and their value should be fully assessed.

A school of the future must have the flexibility to cater for a wide range of users and varying activities including learning and recreational activities, teachers' preparation and meetings involving teachers and other professionals. As the range of educators widens, so do activities and group sizes. Visits from museums or local businesses may involve pupils in different groups, so access to a larger space may be desirable. Flexibility can give users more choice, reflecting the increased value placed on individual needs. This is especially true for pupils with special needs whose requirements vary, both between individuals and from year to year.

One aspect of flexibility is the ability to access different sizes of space. This can be achieved in various ways. Approaches include:

- Making classrooms large enough to cater for a range of different users and activities, avoiding too close a fit to any one space. This 'loose fit' approach tends to increase the overall area

PERTHCELYN PRIMARY SCHOOL, SOUTH WALES
Modular blocks form a podium for assemblies and can be cleared away for dining. Folding doors at the back of the hall can be opened to create the space for a proscenium arch stage or closed to allow music and drama rehearsals.

**DIAGRAMATIC PLAN OF CLASSROOMS
TO SHOW KEY FLEXIBILITY ISSUES**

wall closed

wall open

covered outdoor space used for teaching

circulation space

circulation space used for teaching

●●●●●● covered circulation

—— movable partition

but can be offset against a reduced need to adapt accommodation over time;

- Using moveable partitions between spaces to enable different spaces to be created when needed. These have to be of good quality to withstand heavy school use and are expensive. The detrimental effect on sound insulation should be considered;
- Creating a range of different sized spaces. Rooms are booked as needed by mutual agreement. This should reduce the overall area needed but can be difficult to manage.

Shape, as well as size, can affect the flexibility of a space. It is useful to standardise room proportions as far as possible so that different activities can be accommodated in a number of different spaces. Oddly-shaped spaces which can only be organised in one way should be avoided. Simplicity is usually the key to flexibility, although for some designers this might conflict with efforts to achieve visual excitement through complexity.

It is easier to achieve flexibility where there is little or no need for specialised servicing, furniture or equipment. A secondary science laboratory, for example, has limited alternative use.

Flexibility can be achieved through organisational changes such as adjusting the school timetable or organising group sizes to suit available spaces but the most flexibly designed spaces can only work if building users have a flexible attitude.

FLEXIBILITY AND ADAPTABILITY
A flexible design allows a variety of activities to be accommodated without cost or inconvenience. The level of flexibility required varies according to the building type; thus while the furniture in an individual room in an office building may not be moved for several years, the furniture in a primary classroom may be moved around daily to suit different activities. This definition of flexibility differs from adaptability, which is the ability to adapt a building over time to suit changing needs (see Section 2C.4).

YEWLANDS SECONDARY SCHOOL, SHEFFIELD, CLASSROOM OF THE FUTURE PROJECT
A new flexible learning space links this secondary school's design and technology department with the City Learning Centre. It will be used for group presentations, discussion and private study. Sliding folding partitions allow the main space to be configured as a single open plan area or a series of smaller spaces. The independent structural frame allows future extension and adaptation.

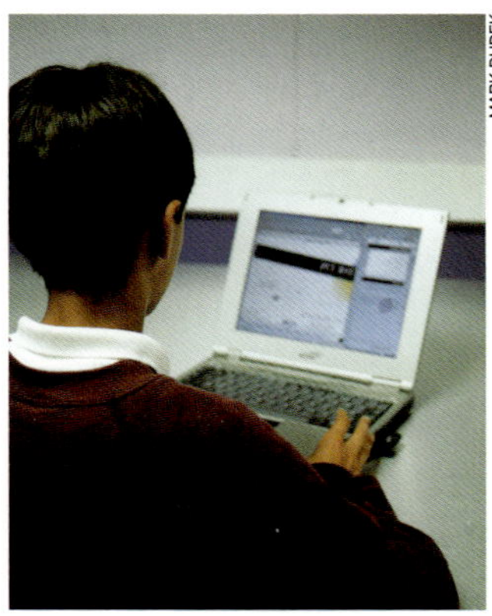

As laptop computers and other portable equipment become more commonplace the space requirements for computing will come down.

Area and balance

- The overall area of schools will be higher than in the past.
- Flexibility is key to making efficient use of available area.

Schools in the future will be focal points for the whole community, providing learning in a variety of ways as well as other services. This is likely to result in an increase in the overall area. While the range of learning spaces will be broadly as now, there will be some changes in the balance of spaces. Accommodation will vary more from school to school, reflecting different approaches.

Building more than the required area will not only require greater initial capital expenditure, but will also lead to higher running costs, in terms of maintenance, cleaning and energy costs for the life of the buildings. In order to make the most efficient use of space, some areas should be designed for dual use.

The number and size of spaces required will be determined by the number and age range of all users and a detailed assessment of the school's curricular and organisational needs (see Building Bulletin 82 for more guidance). It is important that all users and all activities are considered and individual spaces designed with flexibility in mind, as discussed above.

The main influences on the overall area and balance of spaces for a school for the future are summarised below.

ALFRED SALTER PRIMARY SCHOOL, SOUTHWARK, LONDON
This school is designed for inclusion and community use. It is fully accessible by wheelchair, there is an induction loop in the hall and accommodation includes a hygiene room and a room for hearing impaired children. Enhancements to the area to accommodate community use include a larger entrance hall as shown here, a parents' room and a sports changing area.

Curriculum Changes

An increase in vocational courses is likely to have an effect on the area or balance of spaces in only some schools. Links between schools and other learning places will increase, allowing pupils whose school does not have specialised facilities to attend courses at nearby specialist schools, colleges or training centres, or to gain experience at places of work.

New Ways of Learning

An increase in independent learning will have an effect on the balance of spaces. There will be more open access resource areas and there may be more office space for additional support staff and visiting adults. The differences between working and learning space is likely to become blurred. In the short term, an increase in computers could have an impact on area requirements but this is likely to decrease as portable equipment becomes more commonplace. There may be additional specialist resource spaces, for example for video conferencing.

Blurring the Boundaries

Having more people using school facilities during the school day is likely to increase the area required. Some individual spaces may be larger due to enhanced specification (for example, a sports hall to suit competition standards). Dedicated community rooms may be added to the range of spaces. Accommodation for services such as health care will be additional to the core school facility.

However, the pressure on area due to incoming learners should be balanced with the fact that there may be fewer pupils on site at any one time as they increasingly learn off site (see Section 1.2 on variety of learning experience). Different timetabling arrangements such as staggered arrival and leaving times could also reduce the number of pupils on site.

Inclusion

Making schools more inclusive affects the overall area and range of spaces required in a number of ways. The need for additional adult support, whether from teachers, educational psychologists or social workers has clear space implications in the classroom and other areas. The following also have an effect on area:

- Increased movement space for pupils with physical disabilities, particularly wheelchair users;
- Additional specialist support spaces such as therapy rooms;
- Larger or more specialised toilet areas.

Building Bulletin 94 looks at the effects of inclusion on school design in more detail.

Group spaces clockwise from far left: science laboratory (Jersey College for Girls, Jersey); music room; and primary class base (Alfred Salter School, Southwark, London).

2A.1 GROUP SPACES

▶ primary class bases ▶ secondary general learning spaces ▶ practical spaces ▶ spaces with specialist equipment ▶ seminar rooms

- Group spaces will continue to be essential learning spaces.
- Group spaces will be slightly bigger than current recommendations.

Group spaces are where learners are organised into a group, although they won't usually spend an entire session learning as a whole group.

While a typical group size is 20 to 30, sizes will vary from, for example, 10 to 15 in a discussion group, to 80 to 90 listening to a talk from a visiting speaker. Group spaces may be general or be serviced and/or equipped for practical activities (such as science) or specialist activities (e.g. music).

Group spaces are likely to continue to be the largest category of space in a school in the future. In theory, individualised learning could result in pupils learning anywhere, accessing information and contributing through ICT with teachers moving around giving support. However, working alongside others is a vital part of learning.

A base is also important, particularly for young children and there will still be a need for presentation and discussion style learning, whether it is to introduce and discuss a project or to have a traditional skills lesson. Practical activities will still need to be catered for with specialist spaces (despite the possibilities of 'virtual' experience).

Group spaces are likely to be larger than current guidance suggests mainly because of the effect of increased inclusion. Types of group space are likely to be similar to those of today but flexibility will be important so that, for example, a larger group space could be created from two smaller spaces when more than one group want to work together or for community use.

The degree to which group spaces are shared by the community, whether during or outside the school day, will vary from school to school. Primary school group spaces (particularly at infant level) are less likely to be shared because of the differences in furniture size and the vulnerability of displays. There may instead be separate spaces designated for community use, for which the design criteria will be similar to those outlined below.

Group spaces for the future should be adequately sized and flexible enough to accommodate a wider range of users and various ways of learning. Consider in particular the range of activities, movement, support staff, ICT and other equipment. These are discussed in more detail below.

NURSERY, WAKEFIELD GRAMMAR SCHOOL, YORKSHIRE
Low level partitions can create spaces for pupils to work and play on their own, within larger group spaces.

It is important to consider the range of activities taking place in group spaces - from practical technology sessions to computer-based research and learning games - some of which require specialist equipment.

Movement

There needs to be space to allow pupils, including those in wheelchairs or with limited mobility, to move safety around the space. Individual working tends to involve more movement as pupils fetch resources or talk to others.

Support staff

Pupils working in smaller groups or on their own still need assistance at least for part of the time and pupils with special needs often require classroom support. There is therefore likely to be more than one adult in the classroom on many occasions.

ICT and other equipment

Space must be allowed for appropriate equipment, including that used by pupils with special needs. The area implications of computers is likely to change as technology develops. The space implications of using video conferencing equipment and interactive whiteboards in classrooms is likely to be neutral (although providing a specialist video conferencing room could add area). Specialist rooms will continue to have particular requirements but an increase in the use of virtual reality for some practical work may reduce the need for equipment. A few schools may have more sophisticated equipment for practical activities associated with vocational courses such as engineering.

Further guidance on various types of group spaces can be found in Building Bulletins 80, 81, 82, 86, 89 and 92.

Range of activities

A range of activities and ways of working need to be accommodated to suit a flexible learning style. This includes working individually or in small groups and taking part in whole group discussions or presentations (by pupils or teacher). The needs of different users must be considered. The choice of furniture and equipment and its arrangement in the space is also a critical factor in the success of the space.

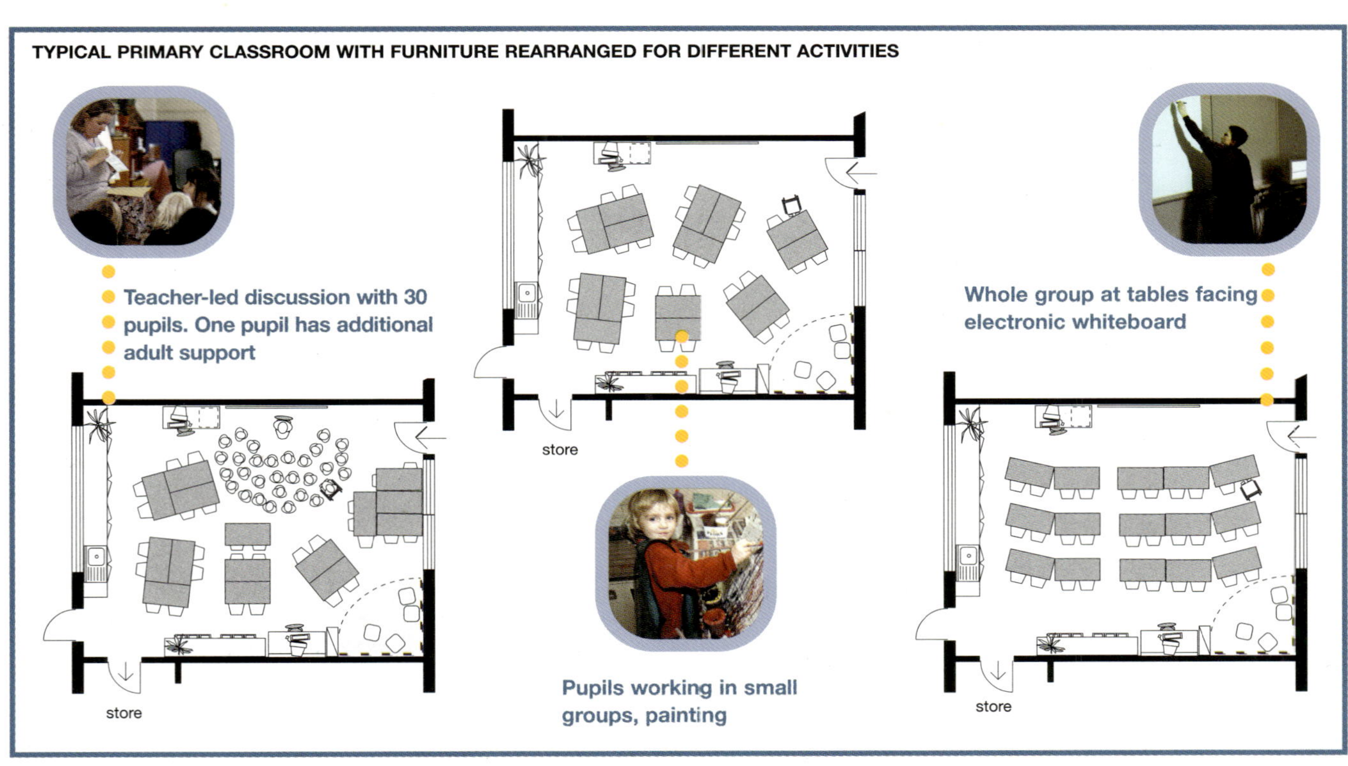

2A.2 LARGE SPACES

▶ gyms ▶ sports halls ▶ dance studios
▶ assembly halls ▶ multi-purpose halls ▶ theatres

- Large spaces will be increasingly used as community resources.
- These spaces take 10 to 20% of the gross area of a school, so they must be justified by reasonable utilisation.

Large spaces tend to be either for large gatherings of people (such as assemblies, meetings, or performances) or for sporting activities. In primary schools such spaces are usually multi-purpose, often being used for dining as well as assembly and PE.

Large spaces are not likely to change significantly in the future, but, as with other school spaces, greater community use and more integration of those with special needs must be considered. Both these factors can affect the area requirement.

The provision of such large spaces (usually over 150m^2 with a minimum ceiling height of 3m and taking up a significant proportion of the overall area of the school) has to be justified by a reasonable use. Schools will increasingly share these spaces with other schools and the community as a whole.

Sports spaces

Sports spaces are likely to continue to have a high level of community use. This can help to provide a sports space for a school that may not otherwise be able to justify such a space (for example a very small primary school). Sports halls used by the community should be large enough to adhere to local competition standards. Community use also affects the nature of supporting spaces and social areas (see Sections 2A.4 and 2A.5).

The needs of physically disabled people may be met by providing multi-use sports spaces designed for a range of activities including those to suit disabled students such as wheelchair basketball. However, in some cases it may be preferable to provide a separate specially-equipped fitness centre.

Meeting and performance spaces

Schools will continue to need space for whole school, year-group assemblies, performances to an audience and (in the case of secondary schools) exams. As these spaces have a number of uses and users, flexibility is essential. For example, removable stage and tiered seating allows for a wider range of uses. Two smaller spaces may be

combined to make a large space for particular occasions.

Community and business use (maybe for film shows or conferences) demands more specialised lighting and environmental controls as well as more sophisticated furniture and finishes.

Further guidance on sports and arts spaces can be found in Sports England publications and Designing Space for Sports and Arts.

ALFRED SALTER PRIMARY SCHOOL, SOUTHWARK, LONDON
Good environmental design, including use of natural daylight, creates an attractive dining environment for pupils, teachers and community members.

ST ANTHONY'S SCHOOL, HAMPSTEAD, LONDON
Large spaces need to be well used by both school and community to justify their area.

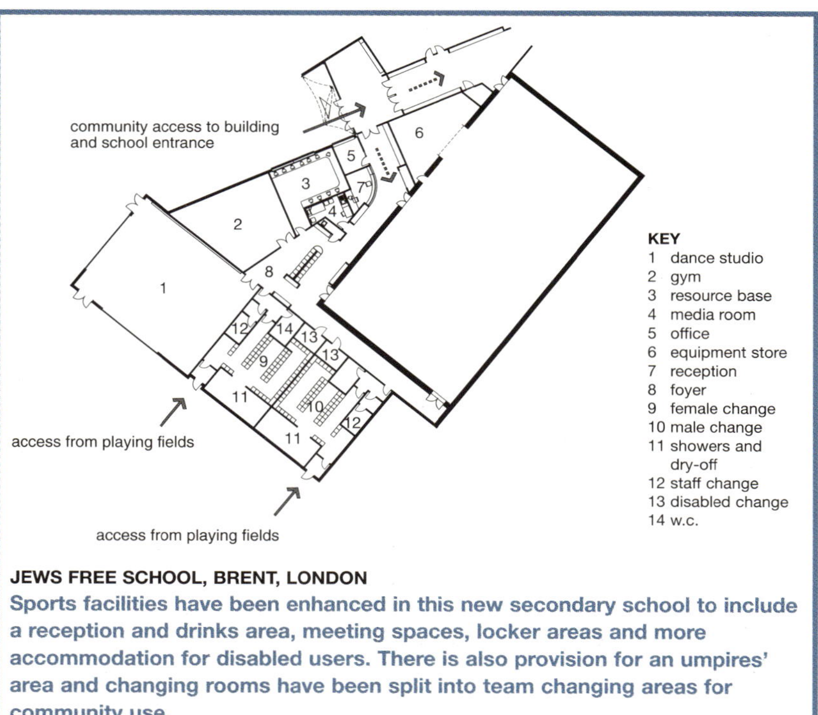

KEY
1 dance studio
2 gym
3 resource base
4 media room
5 office
6 equipment store
7 reception
8 foyer
9 female change
10 male change
11 showers and dry-off
12 staff change
13 disabled change
14 w.c.

JEWS FREE SCHOOL, BRENT, LONDON
Sports facilities have been enhanced in this new secondary school to include a reception and drinks area, meeting spaces, locker areas and more accommodation for disabled users. There is also provision for an umpires' area and changing rooms have been split into team changing areas for community use.

RYDAL SCHOOL, COLWYN BAY,
NORTH WALES
A school's central resource area is vital.

School ICT facilities may be shared with
the community.

2A.3 RESOURCE SPACES

▶ central library/ICT resource ▶ local resource areas ▶ specialist resource areas ▶ study areas ▶ quiet spaces

- These spaces are critical to the success of independent working.
- These spaces should be used flexibly, overlapping with other uses.

Resource areas are spaces where pupils can work away from a large group, both during and out of timetabled hours. They are a critical factor in the success of independent working and so are an important part of the school of the future. Pupils need easy access to places where they can work alone or in small groups. Some level of supervision is likely to be necessary.

Pupils will also spend part of their time working individually in a group space (see above). For some specialist resource areas a booking system may apply, but it is important that a resource area should generally be freely available.

The overlaps between these and other spaces such as social areas and circulation spaces are important if a space is going to be efficiently used. Many of these spaces will also be used by the community. Their size will depend on the age range of pupils, the number of school and community users, and the way in which the school organises its learning.

Central library/ICT resource

A central resource area will continue to be a vital part of any school, although the balance between books and other resources, ICT equipment and study space is now changing and will continue to do so. A central resource area provides a focus for the whole school and can provide a pleasant place for individual study and research, for both school and community.

A library for the future is the central ICT resource housing the school's most sophisticated equipment and software. At secondary level there will also be a number of linked local ICT resource areas around the school (see below). Cybercafés are becoming popular, used by both school and community. The library can also provide the main ICT link between home and school. Some schools may have an additional specialised ICT facility that may be shared with other schools as well as the community.

A library that is used concurrently by the community is likely to be larger than one used solely by the school, in order not to compromise pupil use. There may be a need for more office and storage space and additional furniture and equipment. If the school library

FOREST GATE CITY LEARNING CENTRE,
NEWHAM, LONDON
The specialised ICT facility is used by pupils from other schools and adults during the day and evening (until 7pm); the school can also book space. There are three learning areas and a seminar room, with a total of 60 computers. Each space has an electronic whiteboard and the seminar room has video-conferencing and refreshment facilities. The environment and furniture are of good quality. The centre is accessible from the school's main reception area, minimising disruption to the school and reducing security complications. Those attending courses are issued with identification cards which also act as swipe cards.

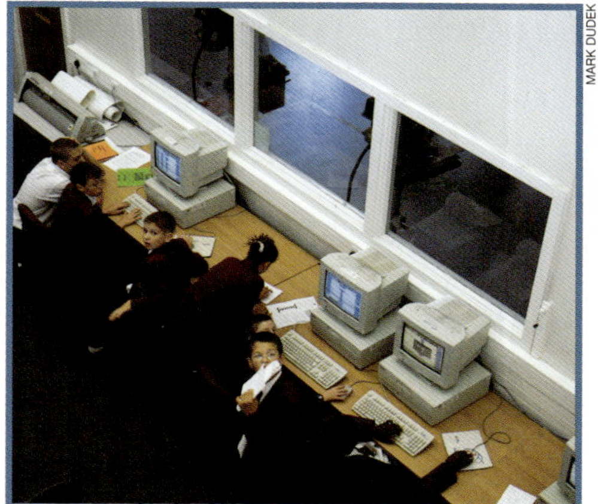

BLENHEIM HIGH SCHOOL, EPSOM, SURREY
This secondary school has been extended and adapted. Local ICT resource areas are provided alongside circulation routes. In the existing building this has been achieved by opening up spaces next to the corridor. In the new extension, resource areas are at nodes along the route (shown here).

QUEEN'S INCLOSURE PRIMARY SCHOOL, WATERLOOVILLE, HAMPSHIRE
This primary school has a very simple rectangular plan. Classrooms are arranged along the north side, offices, hall, cloakrooms on the south. Running down the centre, opening from and overlapping with a central circulation route (and lit by a central rooflight) are alternating quiet enclosed spaces and open resource areas. These provide supplementary space to the class bases. They are attractive well-used areas. The central library and ICT centre is easily accessible from this central area.

doubles as a full community library, accessibility and security are especially important, particularly in a primary school.

Local resource areas

Small shared resource areas already exist to some degree in both primary and secondary schools but they are becoming more crucial for independent working. Local resource spaces may be for general purpose use, with just tables and chairs, or they may be equipped with computers, printers and photocopiers. In a secondary school, they may be linked to a subject area and house relevant resources. These areas may also have more sophisticated ICT (software or hardware) than is available to every pupil, and act as satellites to the central ICT resource area.

Learners may want to work quietly on their own while others may want to take part in small-group discussions with peers. This conflict can be dealt with by careful organising.

Local resource areas will be particularly valuable in secondary schools to those on vocational courses and those spending part of their time studying elsewhere or attending work placements. Open access areas that can double as social spaces, or even refreshment areas, may be a valuable option for non-practical activities to make good use of all available space. Circulation routes can also be designed to accommodate small work bays.

Specialist resource areas

Some independent working requires access to specialist equipment and sometimes technical support. These areas are smaller and more

freely available than specialist group spaces although there is clearly an overlap. A specialist resource area in a secondary school allows students to do practical work in their own time, leave unfinished project work in a safe place, or carry out long-term activities such as data logging.

While unsupervised practical work is possible for activities such as painting, graphics or music, activities such as science experiments require supervision. In some cases, staff may prefer to allow pupils open access to a main group space at agreed times during the day rather than provide a practical resource space. Specialist resource areas in secondary schools are best placed near the subject department.

There is less need for such spaces at primary level where learning spaces tend to be multi-purpose. However, there may be shared

A music resource area can be used for tuition and music practice.

HAYES SCHOOL, BROMLEY, KENT
Open access resource areas promote independent learning.

NORFOLK CLASSROOM OF THE FUTURE PROJECT
Three pilot projects will be developed as part of the Norfolk classroom of the future: three stand-alone classrooms sited at one secondary school (the early design of which is shown here) and two primaries. They will be attempts to develop solutions to the problem of providing and sustaining the educational needs of pupils attending small rural schools, and to counter isolation in such communities. High-tech links will be set up between the primaries and the secondary school to enable, for example, video-conferencing between schools, allowing specialists to teach larger groups or individuals in other schools. The secondary school already has links with schools in France and Germany. The project will also address the existing rural community's general lack of services such as access to banking, libraries, cinemas and so on.

Small spaces are useful for one-to-one teaching, counselling or mentoring.

areas housing equipment that is too expensive to provide in every class base.

The school of the future will make more use of media facilities either for specialist courses or, more generally, for project work. Specialist spaces may also be provided for recording music or drama performances or for assessment purposes. Video-conferencing to other schools or educators will be used more in schools, particularly in rural ones where making visits or attending courses outside school are not easy options. While video conferencing can take place in any group room with appropriate mobile equipment, a central video conferencing room with appropriate acoustic and lighting environment may be provided. This could be combined with a media studio for use by other schools, the community and the business sector. The location and environmental conditions of such spaces have to be carefully thought through.

Quiet spaces

Quiet time needs to be a natural part of the educational environment and there are times when an open resource and work area is not appropriate. Such spaces are increasingly likely to feature in a school of the future as learning becomes more individualised. Pupils need to be able to work undisturbed in a quiet place (usually, but not always an enclosed room) but not feel separated from the main school. Such a place could also satisfy pupils' often expressed desire for places for contemplation.

In a secondary school with a sixth form, there will usually be an area designated for quiet study either attached to the school's central resource centre or in a separate sixth-form base. In many schools, the division between study and social areas has been dropped and pupils work quietly in an area which has access to refreshments (see Section 2A.5 on social and movement spaces). The attractiveness of such a facility may encourage more pupils to stay on into the sixth form. Students should have ready access to ICT, although not all study will require it.

2A.4 SUPPORT SPACES

▶ learning support room ▶ counselling rooms
▶ therapy rooms

■ Support spaces are essential to increase inclusion.
■ Not all support spaces can have shared use.

Support spaces are small spaces for teachers and other professionals to work with individuals or small groups. They are likely to be increasingly used, partly because of greater inclusion (to support but not replace integrated class teaching), and also due to independent working which tends to lead to an increase in the need for occasional individual support. This is particularly true for those with special needs for whom the crucial relationship between student and teacher – that inspires and nurtures learning – cannot always work in public or even in small groups.

Pupils with special needs require assistance from a number of people in addition to their teachers including parents and health and social care professionals. Small spaces are also valuable for counselling and mentoring sessions.

Privacy is important in these rooms and they should be well sound insulated. However, some

ALFRED SALTER PRIMARY SCHOOL, SOUTHWARK, LONDON
Support spaces need to be private, particularly acoustically, but they should also retain visual contact with the rest of the school.

THE QUIET PLACES PROJECT
The University of Liverpool is coordinating a project called 'Quiet Places'. A therapeutic room or 'quiet place' has been set up in 10 Liverpool primary schools, aimed mainly at children with emotional and behavioural difficulties. The project is based on the idea of a holistic approach to personal development, and spaces are run by qualified therapists. The environment is designed to provide a calm place which feels separate from the normal school world. Lighting is muted and masked, colours and furnishings are soft and relaxing, and the acoustics are designed to create stillness.

THE CHARTER SCHOOL, SOUTHWARK, LONDON
This new hall is an example of a multi-purpose gathering and assembly space that acts as a strong statement for the school, close to the main entrance where it can be easily appreciated by visitors as well as pupils.

2A.5 SOCIAL & MOVEMENT

▶ entrance areas ▶ circulation routes
▶ house bases ▶ eating places ▶ social bases
▶ recreation areas ▶ community rooms

■ Attractive social and recreational spaces can improve staff and pupil morale.
■ Entrance areas are important as the public face of the school.

This range of spaces includes places for meetings, eating and socialising for pupils, staff and the community. They are sometimes defined as 'non-learning' spaces but as learning becomes more flexible in the future, the difference between learning and non-learning spaces will become less distinct. There will also be external recreation spaces, these are dealt with below.

This range of spaces is becoming a more important part of a school's accommodation. Attractive and suitable social, recreational and movement areas can:

● Encourage pupils to stay on longer in school;
● Allow more flexible working patterns;
● Improve staff and pupil morale – and thus motivation;
● Support those with special needs;
● Encourage greater community and business use of the school.

These spaces also help inclusion in the broadest sense by providing places for 'escape' and greater independence.

form of visual contact will be needed, for example a vision panel in the door. Many support spaces can overlap with other small spaces such as quiet spaces or offices, given appropriate furniture, but some are too specialised to have an alternative function. For example, the spaces in a learning support centre (a self-contained suite of rooms, supporting pupils with emotional and behavioural difficulties) are unlikely to be used for other purposes. Increased inclusion will result in a greater need for specially furnished and equipped therapy rooms. These range from a space for visiting physiotherapists to work with individual pupils to sensory rooms of varying kinds.

With pupils spending part of their time learning off site the need for a support base at the 'home' school where pupils can meet tutors and access resources may be considered.

Refer to Building Bulletin 94 for further guidance on designing for inclusion.

FIRTH PARK COMMUNITY COLLEGE, LEARNING SUPPORT CENTRE, SHEFFIELD
This comprehensive school provides pupil support in a number of ways (see description in Section 1.4). The SEN staff have a dedicated suite of spaces – classrooms and an office – but they also work alongside teachers in main group rooms. The school is building another dedicated suite for the learning support unit (see plan). It is located centrally but has separate external access.

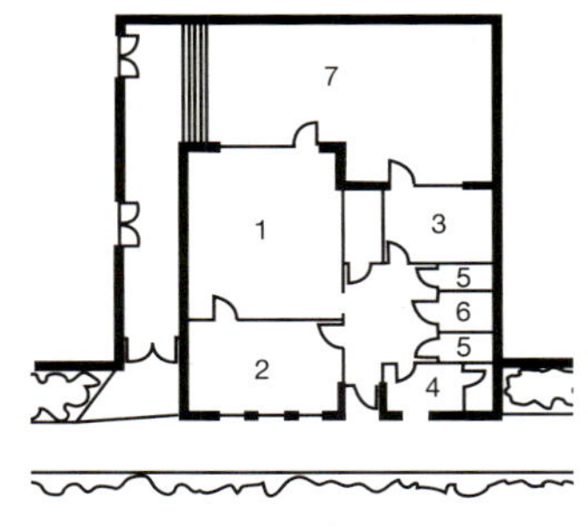

THOMAS TELFORD CITY TECHNOLOGY COLLEGE, TELFORD, SHROPSHIRE
Reception areas should be spacious enough for all users, including those with wheelchairs and pushchairs.

WESTBOROUGH PRIMARY SCHOOL, WESTCLIFF-ON-SEA, ESSEX
Entrance areas can be attractive and welcoming with displays of pupils' work.

CHAFFORD HUNDRED LEARNING CAMPUS, THURROCK, ESSEX
The entrance is a school's public face so it should be clearly visible and attractive.

Entrance areas

The public face of the school is an important part of its success as a learning place for all. The first space that everyone sees on entering the school is the reception area. It is important, particularly if a school is to encourage a wider use of the school's facilities, to make this an attractive and welcoming space. Security should also be considered. Entrances should:

- Have a welcoming and clearly visible reception area;
- Offer opportunities for display of pupils work as well as information that reflects the community nature of the building;
- Have enough movement space for all users including those in wheelchairs and parents with pushchairs.

Circulation areas

Many existing schools have narrow, poorly lit corridors with low ceilings. These spaces are unattractive and lead to congestion and, in the worst cases, behavioural difficulties, which can affect subsequent learning time. The standard of circulation design needs to be improved.

Circulation in school buildings should be designed to cater for a range of users, some of whom will be coming to the school for the first time. There are a number of circulation issues to be considered, including planning, lighting, acoustics and finishes. Environmental matters are covered in Section 2B and planning issues are covered in Section 2C.

More imaginative design can make better use of circulation space creating more varied areas, blurring the edges between space for movement and space for socialising and learning. Wide enough circulation routes can be places where pupils meet as they are getting belongings from their lockers. Corridors can be opened up for use as informal learning areas.

Circulation routes should be wide enough to avoid congestion, taking account of people with disabilities and weight of traffic. Doors need to be positioned to minimise restriction. A view from the corridor into a learning space or outside gives a sense of openness and increases the sense of width. For more detail on circulation issues, refer to Building Bulletins 91 and 94.

ROYAL DOCKS COMMUNITY SCHOOL, NEWHAM, LONDON
This is a fully inclusive school, with provision for those with profound and multiple learning difficulties. There is a lift, but it was felt that all pupils, including those in wheelchairs, should be able to use the same way of moving around. A ramp therefore has been built to form a central feature of the building. Corridors are 2.5m wide to accommodate wheelchairs and glazed screens allow views into all learning bases and add to the feeling of space. On the upper floor the corridors are well lit by daylight.

Social bases

Spaces in which year or house groups can gather can be valuable at secondary level, particularly in large schools where pupils feel a lack of community or where bullying and poor attendance are felt to be partly due to the lack of a social base. As these spaces only have intermittent use, they should have other uses, for example as group rooms or resource areas. Lockers may be kept in social bases. See Section 2A.7 for a discussion on locker location.

In the future, the traditional sixth form social area could be more flexibly used, combining study and social functions.

Parent/community rooms

Many schools already have social and recreational spaces that are solely for community use. As schools become more open to the community such places will become more commonplace. There may be a space that parents and carers can call their own, a comfortable, welcoming room where they can meet staff or other parents. This or another space may be used by parents of special needs pupils for discussions with teachers and carers and, where appropriate, to learn how to help their child access certain equipment, and other tools for learning.

Eating spaces

The typical secondary school dining hall is a noisy and institutional space that is uninviting to everyone. As dining tends to be concentrated into a short period, the lunch hour becomes very congested and yet the space is rarely used for other purposes when empty. Tables and chairs are usually functional but unattractive.

An attractive café-style space that is open all day is more appropriate for a modern learning environment, bringing together pupils, community users and staff. It can become the social centre of the school, where parents meet their children and mentors talk to pupils. Longer opening hours will allow pupils to work more flexibly, with less rigid break times, easing congestion at lunch time and possibly reducing the area need. A café can also provide an additional area for informal independent working, making better use of available areas. This blurring of the boundary between work and recreation or refreshment reflects a trend in office planning where staff are encouraged to meet and work away from their usual environment.

The size of an eating space will need to take account of the number of people using it at any one time, including adult community users and those in wheelchairs. Good environmental

KINGSDALE SECONDARY SCHOOL, SOUTHWARK, LONDON
A consultation process (see Section 3.2) revealed that pupils wanted a social base where they could feel at home. The school has now been organised into houses, each of which will have a base. To make best use of accommodation these will double as teaching bases but will be less heavily timetabled than other spaces.

WESTBOROUGH PRIMARY SCHOOL, ESSEX
Westborough Primary School's after-school club doubles as a community room for parents' meetings and other events. There are tea- and coffee-making facilities and toilets in the building so it can be used independently of the rest of the school. Folding doors open on to a garden area.

WALTON HIGH, MILTON KEYNES, BUCKINGHAMSHIRE
An attractive eating space in the heart of the school.

BA WATERSIDE CENTRE, HILLINGDON, LONDON
The building was built in 1998 as British Airways' head office. It was designed as an office of the future with 'hot desking' and minimal paper use. Staff are encouraged to use the cafés in this central street where informal meetings and individual working take place throughout the day. It is attractive, with natural finishes evoking an external environment flooded with daylight. Such an approach is influencing modern school design.

GAINSBOROUGH ADVENTURE PLAYGROUND, GAINSBOROUGH, LINCOLNSHIRE
A colourful café-style facility for the whole community.

design is vital to its success.

Smaller, additional refreshment areas can be considered for a secondary school, particularly if a school is running a more flexible timetable. These spaces can provide informal meeting and working areas for pupil or adult use. This is particularly appropriate adjacent to sports facilities where there is significant community use.

Catering facilities at primary schools should also provide an attractive dining environment which is open longer, accommodating community as well as pupil needs (study support often occurs at breakfast time or after school). Because eating usually takes place in a multi-purpose hall in a primary school, it is difficult to make the space available to the community throughout the day. An additional refreshment facility for community use, adjacent to the main school catering facilities, providing light refreshments may be useful. A kitchen for the community's own use could also be considered.

2A.6 STAFF AREAS

▶ central staff work rooms ▶ departmental bases ▶ staff social areas ▶ teachers' offices ▶ administrative offices ▶ support staff offices

- Teaching staff need space in which to work during their non-contact time.
- There will be more adults doing a greater variety of tasks in schools.
- The division between work and social space is blurring.

A school of the future should provide suitable and attractive social and working facilities for all staff whether teachers or administrators, or those giving educational, technical or medical support. The needs of professionals based in linked facilities such as health centres must also be considered. A good learning environment is important for the recruitment and motivation of staff. Although this section focuses specifically on staff areas, staff needs should be considered when designing all school accommodation. Classroom teaching is only part of a teacher's job. The working environment should enable teachers to perform a range of non-contact activities including lesson planning, marking, meeting with colleagues and management. Privacy and quiet will often be required. Staff should also have access to a quiet rest room.

Staff accommodation requirements, including departmental staff bases, offices and social areas, will vary between schools, and the size of local and central staff areas must be planned to account for the number of users.

DIXONS CITY TECHNOLOGY COLLEGE, BRADFORD, WEST YORKSHIRE
This City Technology College for 1000 pupils, built in 1990, has a series of wings opening off a central mall. At one end of the mall, adjacent to the main entrance and opening off the main restaurant, is an informal café-style eating area for snacks and drinks. It can be used at all times of the day and is easily reached by visitors. Furniture is lightweight and modern, adding to the sense of informality.

SIR GEORGE MONOUX SIXTH FORM COLLEGE, WALTHAMSTOW, LONDON
An attractive eating and social space can be used for informal staff meetings.

CLEVEDEN SECONDARY SCHOOL, GLASGOW
This is a major refurbishment and extension project, part of a city-wide PFI project. The pre-existing school had a traditional central staff room, but it was decided that better use could be made of the available space if it was replaced by departmental staff bases. These bases have work places with ICT provision as well as refreshment facilities. Staff are adjusting to the new idea. In order to prevent isolation they plan to arrange regular all-staff social events.

There should be spaces for teachers to meet with colleagues.

Consideration should be given to the amount of time staff spend in individual offices as sharing is often appropriate. There can be overlaps in some staff areas between staff and pupil use as long as privacy and security are assured. Whatever the arrangement, access to networked ICT and a telephone is essential for all staff. There will also need to be areas for secure filing and personal storage.

A wider range and greater number of support staff are being deployed in schools which has implications for their accommodation, network access, personal storage, recreation spaces and access to the staff with whom they work. Peripatetic staff can share staff areas and the school refreshment facilities but a separate area may be considered for adults such as visiting speakers.

Some secondary schools are now experimenting with doing away with the central staff room, providing only local departmental offices. There is also a trend (as with pupil areas) towards merging social and work spaces.

2A.7 SERVICE SPACES

▶ toilets and hygiene rooms ▶ changing areas
▶ storage ▶ kitchens ▶ ICT support spaces

- Better quality toilets can raise pupil morale.
- Special educational needs must be considered in all service spaces.
- Adult provision should be sufficient for all staff and for community users.

Service spaces are core facilities that support the main school spaces. They are often neglected but they should be given full consideration.

Toilets, hygiene areas and changing
School toilets are the subject of much discontent amongst pupils, affecting their self-esteem. Problems include too many units in a group; poor maintenance; poor ventilation and undersized cubicles. Usage patterns must be considered as toilets are heavily used for a limited period (this applies also to staff toilets). However this may become less of an issue with a more flexible timetable. There should be adequate provision for adults including peripatetic staff and visiting community users. The needs of disabled pupils and adults will need to be taken into account and in some cases this will require hygiene suites.

Changing facilities associated with sport and maybe drama activities must take into account both community and special needs users. The standard of accommodation may need to be enhanced to suit extensive community use.

'Clean toilets that lock, with soap, and flushes not chains'

Children's Manifesto, the Guardian's 'School I'd Like' competition

FAR LEFT:
ST GEORGE'S SCHOOL, EDINBURGH
Attractive spaces for meetings and recreation can help motivate staff.

LEFT:
NURSERY, WAKEFIELD SCHOOL, YORKSHIRE
Functional, high-quality toilets must take the user into account.

GAINSBOROUGH ADVENTURE PLAYGROUND, GAINSBOROUGH, LINCOLNSHIRE
Both long-term storage and local, accessible storage need to be provided to keep main spaces clutter-free.

CATERHATCH INFANT SCHOOL, LONDON
Personal belongings need to be kept clear of classroom activity.

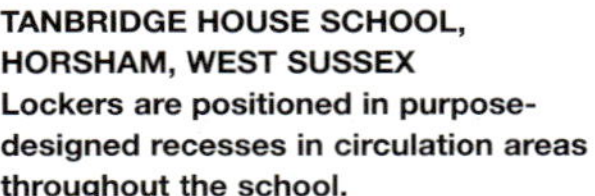

TANBRIDGE HOUSE SCHOOL, HORSHAM, WEST SUSSEX
Lockers are positioned in purpose-designed recesses in circulation areas throughout the school.

HAYES SCHOOL, BROMLEY, KENT
A confusing collection of school buildings has been unified with a new glazed circulation route. The colonnade acts as a promenade and houses lockers, visibility and accessibility making security less problematic. The clusters of lockers also act as informal social gathering spaces as pupils fetch their belongings.

Storage

Schools need to store teaching materials and equipment as well as personal belongings and storage needs are changing. There are fewer books but more equipment, including that for those with special needs. An increase in community use in the future will necessitate additional and separate storage, for example to store equipment used only by adults. The location of storage areas is important (see planning, Section 2C).

Teaching storage is often neglected but it is essential to provide for it adequately in order to ensure learning spaces are kept clear and are more flexible in use. Providing adequate storage space also reduces the risk of unsafe areas such as plant rooms being used for storage. The quantity and type of storage will need assessment in conjunction with users. Both long term storage and local accessible storage need to be considered. If laptop computers are used they will need to be stored securely in a place where they can be recharged, unless pupils take them home. Pupils with special needs may have specialist ICT or other equipment which will need to be stored when not in use.

Pupils personal belongings need to be kept clear of classroom activity and circulation spaces. In primary schools coats and bags are normally kept close to pupils' class bases. In secondary schools there may be central storage (whether in lockers off circulation areas or racks in cloakrooms) or local storage in learning spaces. The former avoids pupils carrying heavy bags between classes. Whatever system is used, coats and bags should be secure and accessible without causing disruption to classes or congestion. Physically disabled pupils may have wheelchairs or other mobility aids that need storing when not in use.

DUKERIES COMPLEX, OLLERTON, NOTTINGHAMSHIRE
The original school was built in 1964 as an 1800-place comprehensive. In 1984 surplus accommodation was adapted to make a community centre for an isolated rural ex-mining community. 2000 adults enrol each year for adult education courses, many of which are linked to the school's sixth form. In addition to the main educational provision there are other services sharing the site including: under 5s; youth centre; day centre for the elderly; leisure centre; centre for adults with learning difficulties; public library; fire training centre. Office space is rented out to services including the probation service and the registrar of births, marriages and deaths.

2A.8 OTHER SERVICES

▶ health centres ▶ social services ▶ Citizens Advice Bureaux ▶ business suite ▶ Sure Start Centre ▶ crèche

■ Schools will increasingly share their site with other services.

In the future, there are likely to be a range of other agencies sharing the school site. Accommodation may range from an office within the school to a separate but linked facility such as a health centre or bank. These facilities are not discussed in detail here but some relevant planning matters are covered in Section 2C.

If there is a crèche (for school staff or parents attending classes or using other facilities on site), access and security must be considered as well as the link to the early years area of the school, where necessary.

Further guidance on designing early years facilities can be found in Designing For 3 to 4 Year Olds. There are also some references to accommodation needs in the National Standards for Under Eights Day Care and Childminding.

2A.9 EXTERNAL AREAS

▶ sports facilities ▶ learning areas ▶ recreation areas ▶ landscaped areas

■ External spaces can present a positive image to the community.
■ Secondary schools could use external spaces more imaginatively.

Schools today are often set back from the road and surrounded by large expanses of tarmac. This does not give a favourable impression to pupils,

KETTLETHORPE HIGH SCHOOL, WAKEFIELD, YORKSHIRE
As part of its extension and reorganisation, a French-style café was created for use by the modern foreign languages department. Outside the café a courtyard is used for eating in fine weather. Both areas are also used by others as social bases.

VICTORIA INFANTS SCHOOL, SANDWELL
The school's community room is regularly used as a crèche.

GRANDVIEW UUQINAK'UH COMMUNITY SCHOOL, VANCOUVER, CANADA
This urban primary school wanted to increase people's experience of open space. The school's external space is intended to serve a range of functions: social (a place where neighbours can socialise); ecological (to educate people about gardening and earth sciences); and economic (a space for growing food). Features include community garden plots; an outdoor meeting room; play areas; and wildflower, butterfly and hummingbird gardens.

WHITELEY PRIMARY, FARNHAM, HAMPSHIRE
Around the school a woodland walk has been devised to provide direct educational experience and a beautiful backdrop to pupils' learning experience, as part of the Learning through Landscapes concept developed in Hampshire.

TANBRIDGE HOUSE SCHOOL, HORSHAM, WEST SUSSEX
Tanbridge House design and technology workshop has an outside semi-covered area for noisy, dusty or messy work. Such a space can also be used for large scale projects and three dimensional art work.

staff or community users.

Tomorrow's schools should have a pleasant external environment designed with the full range of users in mind. Welcoming surroundings have a positive effect on the experience of the school's regular users as well as attracting community and business users to the school premises.

External spaces should be an integral part of the design. Proper planning and landscaping of these spaces is important not just for aesthetic reasons but also because parts of the curriculum including, of course, sport, can be delivered in school grounds at both primary and secondary level (see Building Bulletins 71, 82, 85 and 94).

Access routes, car parking and other such areas are considered in Section 2C.2.

Outside learning spaces

Outside space can provide a stimulating alternative learning environment for all ages, and is an important part of broadening the educational experience. For the under fives, physical experience is a valuable component of learning. Being involved with the upkeep of the grounds can be part of a learning experience.

PITMORE SPECIAL SCHOOL, EASTLEIGH, HAMPSHIRE
Pitmore is a school for pupils with emotional and behavioural difficulties. The garden provides a safe and structured alternative to the classroom and is used regularly for therapeutic work. Withdrawn children can benefit from calm activities like planting or harvesting; the continuity of growth from seed to flower helps develop trust of adults and care for the environment. Digging, cutting down nettles and rushing around with wheelbarrows are therapeutic ways to let out frustrations.

BRIDGWATER COLLEGE, EARLY YEARS CENTRE, SOMERSET
As an extra-curricular activity, the Children's Centre offers a forest school experience to children over three years old. Within a secure woodland environment children can move away from close adult supervision and experience a sense of freedom, so becoming more responsible for each other and themselves. A semi-permanent shelter has been built in the woods and a lock-up cabin houses the portable toilet and tools and equipment. The Danish model, on which the forest school is based, is designed to encourage young children's appreciation of the natural environment and responsibility for conservation in later life.

The area outside the primary classroom is already much used as an extension to the class base and there have been exciting uses made of primary school grounds for learning, whether as planted areas or large scale learning experiences. At secondary level this area of experience has been neglected with the possible exception of using external hard-surfaced areas for some practical work.

Whatever the age group, it is useful to provide some areas that are sheltered from the weather. Security must also be considered, particularly for the under fives.

Sports facilities

Minimum areas for playing fields on which team games can take place are set out in the Education (School Premises) Regulations (1999). Areas are based on the numbers of pupils at the school and their ages, but only apply to schools which have pupils over the age of eight. Where playing fields are grassed, they must be capable of sustaining at least seven hours a week of games. Some types of all-weather surfaces, such as hard porous, synthetic and polymeric surfaces, can be counted as twice their actual area for the purposes of the regulations.

A school of the future may have more generous provision to encourage greater participation in sport at all ages and to cater for increased out of hours and community use. Both grassed and hard surfaced areas are needed to ensure a range of skills can be developed. Playing fields must be able to sustain the impact of much more than seven hours a week usage if they are to benefit participants of all ages. This points to an increasing provision of all-weather pitches and running tracks, matched where appropriate with floodlighting (see Building Bulletin 85 for information on the sizes of pitches and tracks). Provision for the performing arts may also be considered as a part of the school landscape. This could also function as a social space.

Recreation areas

Recreation areas are an important part of any school. In urban areas, the school grounds may be a pupil's main experience of outside space. These areas should be attractively designed and full of variety of space. Some people will want quiet enclosed places for contemplation or talking with friends. Some will want open spaces where they can run about or play team games. Outside areas can also provide alternative places to eat in fine weather. Pupils with SEN have particular access and sensory needs (see Building Bulletin 94). There should be some shelter from the weather.

COOMBES INFANT AND NURSERY SCHOOL, READING, BERKSHIRE
The school grounds are used in all curriculum areas. In the playground, contrast and variety of experience help children learn. Coloured markings define areas and shapes. There is provision for chess, hopscotch and snakes and ladders, as well as a numbered grid and a Schlegel mathematical figure. Markings are reinforced by other features for play, such as fixed tyres to climb on, a boat and a concrete humpbacked bridge. 'Shells' form protected enclaves for storytelling.

In the future schools may have more generous playing-field provision to encourage participation across a range of users.

THE WESTBOROUGH PRIMARY SCHOOL, WESTCLIFF-ON-SEA, ESSEX
Recreation areas should include a variety of spaces for different activities.

SWANLEA SECONDARY SCHOOL, TOWER HAMLETS, LONDON
This secondary school built in the East End of London is on a tight urban site. The school centres around a mall that runs the length of the site from east to west, effectively dividing the site. On the north side are the sports facilities and car parking. On the south side is a landscaped recreational area in a series of courtyards. Interest is provided through variety; there are paved play areas, formal gardens and an ecological area with a pond.

**LILLIPUT NURSERY, ST ALBANS
CATHOLIC PRIMARY SCHOOL, ESSEX**

GROVE ROAD PRIMARY, HOUNSLOW

2B THE LEARNING ENVIRONMENT

This section looks at environmental design in the broadest sense, including the sensory environment (light, air, sound) and the aesthetic side (furniture, fixtures and finishes and the external environment). A good learning environment should be functional, humane and attractive. By raising pupil and staff morale such an environment can have a number of benefits, including contributing towards more effective working, reducing poor behaviour; and encouraging older pupils to stay on at school. It will also encourage community and business use, and adults returning to education. A stimulating environment can also particularly help very young children learn and promote design awareness.

Users like to feel that they are in control of their environment. All user controls (for example for ventilation) should therefore be easily comprehensible and accessible. This section is divided into the five following areas:

2B.1   Lighting
2B.2   Acoustics
2B.3   Heating, ventilation and water
2B.4   Finishes, fixtures and landscape
2B.5   Furniture

Positive places

The following links have been suggested by studies into the relationship between the environment and learning, particularly in relation to pupils with special educational needs or disabilities.

- When asked what they like about an environment, most children mention colour, light and space.
- Natural light, or wide-spectrum high frequency fluorescent lighting is preferable to low frequency (50Hz) fluorescent lighting.
- The use of yellow, beige or off-white surface colours can stimulate learning while light blue, green and lavender can be calming, but some vibrant colours can over-excite and have a negative effect on learning.
- Certain scents can aid problem solving, for example peppermint, basil and lemon can stimulate thinking while lavender, camomile and rose can relax and calm.

These findings, however, cannot be universally applied as individuals react differently to their environment. For example, some learners find concentration, understanding and recall enhanced by background music, while others require total silence. For more information see Building Bulletin 94.

GLASTONBURY THORN SCHOOL, BUCKINGHAMSHIRE
Daylight and ventilation is brought into the deep plan of this school by generous sun pipes which are supplemented by both uplighting and downlighting. Shared working spaces and the hall for gym are both lit by this combination.

SWANLEA SECONDARY SCHOOL, TOWER HAMLETS, LONDON
The quality of daylight is an important part of the design. On upper floors, classrooms have high curved ceilings and tall windows letting in plenty of daylight and creating attractive learning spaces. The central mall is flooded with light through a curved glazed roof, where prismatic glass allows in low winter sun but reflects most of the summer sun. Glazing between classrooms and the mall provides some borrowed light into the back of classrooms, and more importantly a view into classrooms.

2B.1 LIGHTING

- Good lighting can significantly enhance a space.
- Electric lighting will become more important as schools are open longer hours.

Good lighting is important in schools for functional reasons and because it can have a powerful effect on the atmosphere of a space. Daylight should be the principle means of illumination where possible (this is especially important for visual disciplines such as art). Variety and interest should be aimed for rather than an even flat light. The use of windows to 'open out' the school to surrounding views is also important. Any special needs of pupils and other users should be taken into account. Building Bulletins 87 and 90 cover daylighting and electric lighting in some detail.

A space can be considered well daylit if it has an average daylight factor of 4-5% and a uniformity ratio of 0.3-0.4. Key factors in achieving this are the position and area of glazing, ceiling height and depth of space. Daylighting should therefore be considered at the earliest planning stage. Consider, for example, the difficulty of getting daylight to the back of rooms over 6m deep if there are windows on only one side; the use of courtyards to bring daylight (and ventilation) into deep plan building; avoidance of narrow gaps between buildings which can

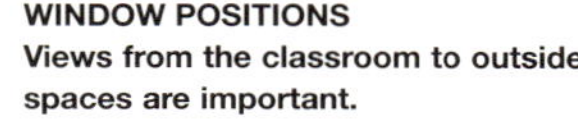

WINDOW POSITIONS
Views from the classroom to outside spaces are important.

CHILDSPLAY NURSERY, HAYLING ISLAND, HAMPSHIRE
The nursery accommodates 40 babies and children from 0-5. It comprises two playrooms with a dining area between. These spaces face south and get additional daylight from clerestory glazing along the north side. A deep roof overhang shades the spaces from summer sun and provides a sheltered play area. Natural light is sufficient to avoid the need for electric lighting for most of the year and gives the play spaces a restful, pleasant atmosphere.

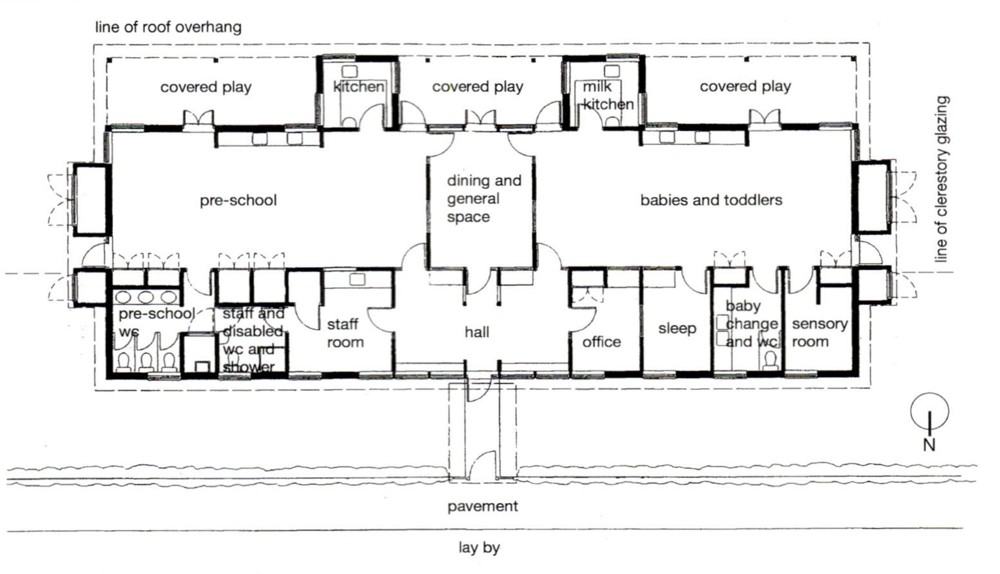

KEY DAYLIGHTING CONSIDERATIONS

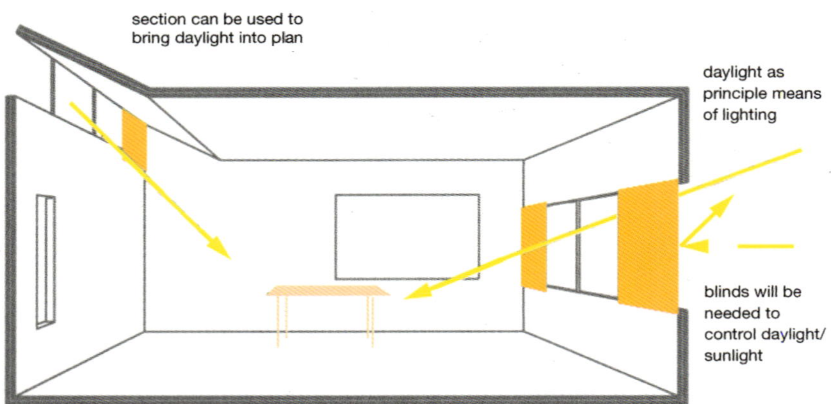

reduce available daylight. Light-coloured reflective surfaces both inside and out can also make a significant contribution to daylight levels.

Window blinds are essential for good viewing of a whiteboard or screen (laptop, full size PC screen or electronic whiteboard). They need not give a complete blackout but must screen out direct sunlight. Blinds or some other method of shading will be needed in any space where direct sunlight penetration is likely. Dedicated video-conferencing rooms and most performance spaces will require blackout facilities (and good acoustic conditions).

Good electric lighting is just as important as daylighting particularly as extended opening hours will mean an increased reliance on it. The recommended background lighting levels given in Building Bulletin 87 (350 lux in general

WOODLEA PRIMARY SCHOOL, BORDON, HAMPSHIRE
Woodlea is set in a beautiful landscape. The materials for the building have been carefully chosen. The 'outer crust' of the building is of multi-yellow rough stock bricks while the softer inner areas are timber-framed, with natural timber ceilings, giving a totally different feel. Terracotta floor tiles in classrooms each have themed patterned insets designed by guest artists. High standards of natural lighting have been achieved by means of patent glazed roof lights, clerestorey windows and lanterns.
White-painted sloping ceilings reflect daylight into classrooms and uplighters give even, glare-free lighting. Electric lighting is only required on the dullest of days in the main teaching areas and hall.

GREAT BINFIELD PRIMARY SCHOOL, BASINGSTOKE, HAMPSHIRE
This 200-pupil new primary school is designed to include pupils with a variety of special needs including visual impairment. Environmental features include:
- A well-lit reception desk positioned clearly to help visually-impaired pupils;
- Contrasting colours to emphasise different surfaces, for example columns in contrast to floors at the entrance;
- High frequency fluorescent lighting to avoid flicker and glare. North light is used to minimise glare and blinds and overhangs control direct sunlight;
- Low reflective finishes on surfaces;
- Few doors - where they exist they have features like contrast colour handles;
- Reduced numbers of obstacles, dropped kerbs and underfloor heating means that radiators are not required.

teaching areas and 500 lux for detailed work such as painting) should not be exceeded. If more light is needed for a specific purpose it is best to provide task lights.

Luminaires with specular-type louvres are not needed for computers except perhaps in dedicated computer suites. Uplighting and wall-wash lights can be used to illuminate the ceilings and walls. Good lighting is especially important for lip-reading and downlighting should be avoided because of the shadows it casts. A dimming facility provides flexibility and is particularly useful for lights close to an electronic whiteboard. External lighting is important for building security and the safety of occupants, particularly as evening use increases. Emergency lighting may be needed for out of hours community use.

TULSE HILL PRIMARY SCHOOL, LAMBETH, LONDON
A Royal Society of Arts grant has provided a lighting designer and artist, who has used features such as coloured light in corridors to provide interest. The lighting scheme will also keep the school lit up, so 'alive' for the community for much of the day.

CHAFFORD HUNDRED LEARNING CAMPUS, THURROCK, ESSEX
Good environmental conditions - achieved as far as possible by natural means – has been a key part of the design. Classrooms have higher than average ceilings and south facing classrooms are shielded from the highest sun by brise soleil. Terraces are light in colour to reflect light into ground floor classrooms. High mass building elements are used to reduce summer heat gain. Naturally cool air is circulated in the building overnight and used for cooling during the day. Ventilation chimneys at the rear of classrooms extract naturally warm air.

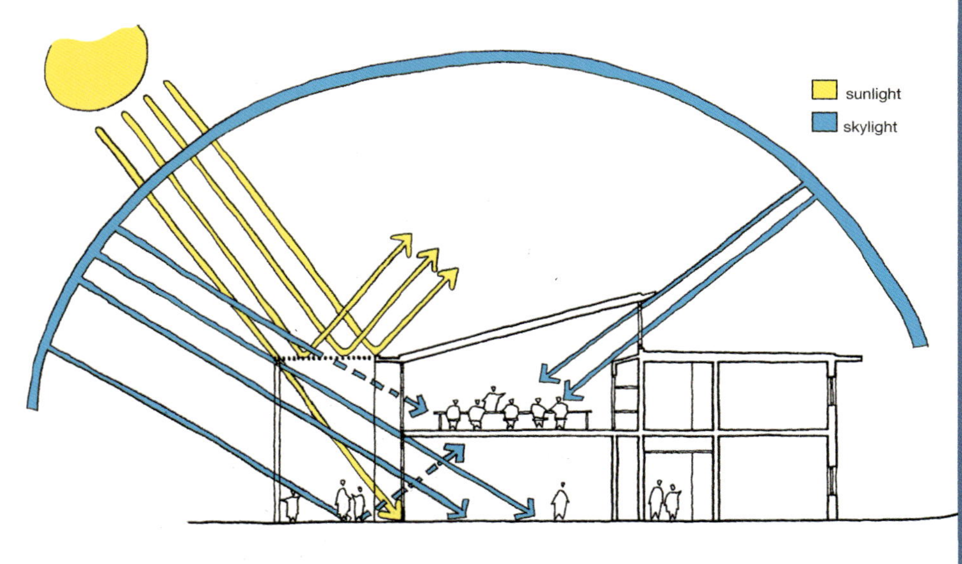

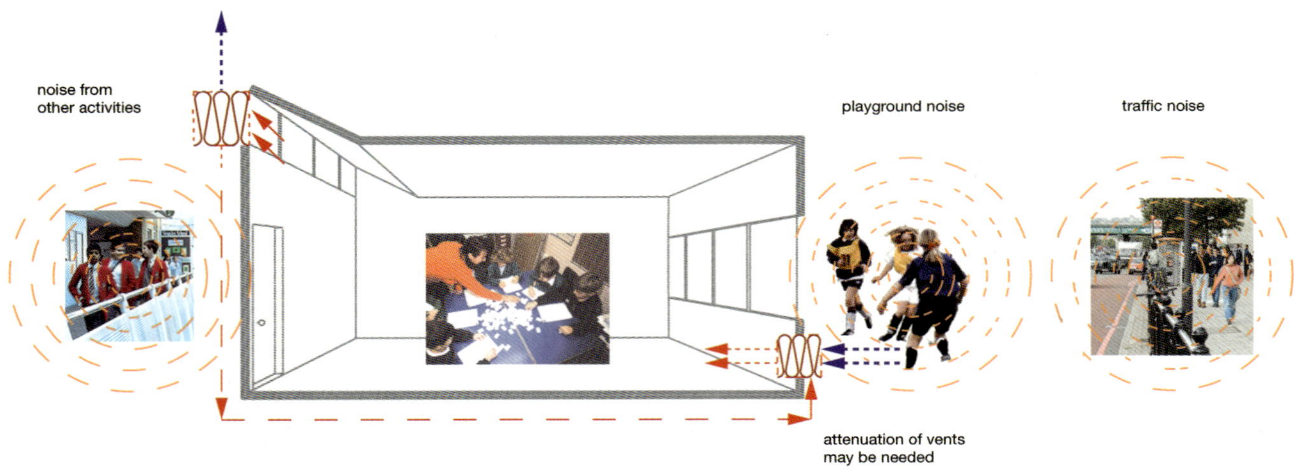

KEY ACOUSTIC CONSIDERATIONS AT DESIGN STAGE

THE BURTON BOROUGH SCHOOL, NEWPORT, SHROPSHIRE
In this secondary school's specialist music centre individual volumes are used for different rooms to ensure acoustic separation.

2B.2 ACOUSTICS

- Enclosed spaces are needed for activities such as whole-class presentations where a relatively low background noise level is essential.
- The needs of the hearing impaired should be considered.

Good acoustics are essential for learning, and adequate sound insulation is necessary for activities such as music. An increase in inclusion, particularly of pupils with hearing and visual impairments, is likely to lead to the adoption of more stringent standards and the needs of community users, especially the elderly, should be considered. For more acoustic guidance, see Building Bulletins 94, 93 and 89.

Speech intelligibility is very important to understanding. For good intelligibility, speech should be at least 10 decibels above background noise level at the listener's ear (higher if learners have hearing impairments). Presentations and discussions with a group of pupils or quiet study, obviously need far better sound insulation than more informal individual or group work. For this reason there will always be a need for some enclosed spaces in a school. Open plan areas can be very successful but only for some activities and they rely on a reasonable level of behaviour by occupants to avoid disturbance.

As noisy activities can disturb quiet ones, the location of spaces should be considered at planning stage. The design of the external envelope should limit noise intrusion (problems include traffic and even rain noise).

As noisy activities can disturb quiet ones, the location of such spaces should be carefully considered.

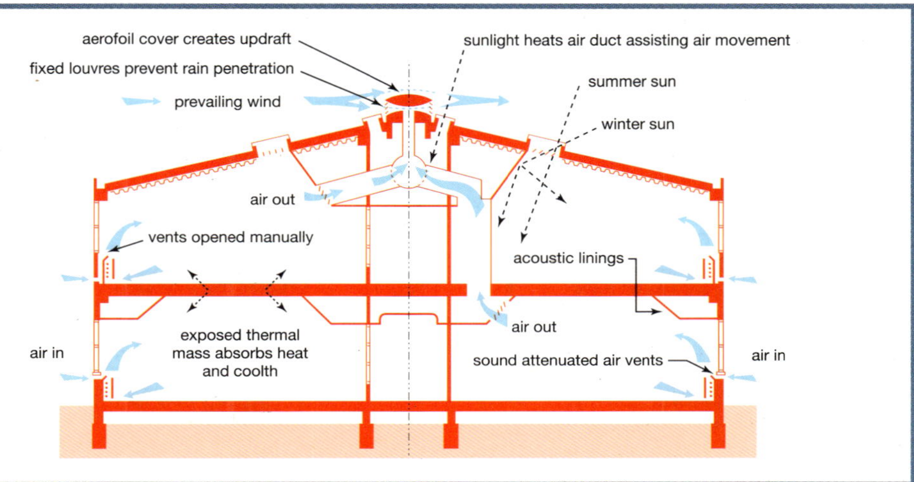

ROYAL DOCKS COMMUNITY SCHOOL, NEWHAM, LONDON
The affect of high ambient noise levels from traffic outside has been reduced by the introduction of fresh air into rooms via acoustically-attenuated inlets. Used air is drawn out of the rooms to roof level in vertical air ducts (with more acoustic insulation). This stack effect ensures ventilation when it is warm and when there is a wind. The profiled metal deck roof is acoustically filled above partition wall.

HAUTE VALLEE SCHOOL, JERSEY
Stack ventilation through the 'chimneys' on the roof of the building keeps fresh air circulating around the school.

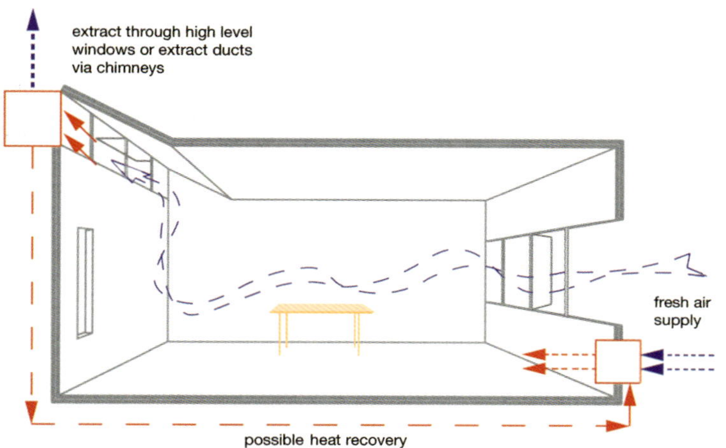

VENTILATION DESIGN: NATURAL, MECHANICAL AND HYBRID SYSTEMS

2B.3 HEATING, VENTILATION AND WATER

- Aim for natural ventilation where possible.
- Balance the comfort needs of those with special needs and others.

A school of the future should provide a comfortable and even temperature with a good level of ventilation for all its users including those with special needs. Guidance is provided in Building Bulletin 87.

While natural ventilation is preferable, studies have shown that school users often don't open windows as needed to provide adequate ventilation. Therefore automatically opened vents and windows may be needed. To avoid this complication and to prevent ventilation heat losses, some form of mechanical ventilation has been advised by some designers; controls should be made easy and comfortable to work. This may also be an issue in a built-up area where opening a window results in noise and poor air quality.

Good indoor air quality in schools is a key design issue. A good target is between 1,000 and 1,500 parts per million of carbon dioxide in the indoor air. For classrooms which are densely occupied, this implies an air change rate of 8 litres per person per second of fresh air, considerably above the standard minimum requirement.

Good ventilation is important in toilets. Wall type combined extract and supply fans are now available to assist with heat recovery and should be used in preference to normal extract-only fans.

Air conditioning is not generally required in schools and should be avoided because of its high cost and energy consumption. It may be needed locally in some existing schools where there is a high concentration of ICT and poor control of external and internal heat gains. This should not be necessary in a well designed new school using thermal mass and night ventilation. Computer servers produce a lot of heat but can withstand higher temperatures than people and may be located in separate areas. Flat screen technology is reducing the heat load caused by computers.

Some SEN pupils require different room temperatures and levels of ventilation which can be difficult where a variety of users are present. It is generally better to err on the cool side, although some SEN pupils may need to keep warm due to lack of mobility or some other medical reason. Refer to Building Bulletin 87 for more information.

Drinking water supplied from the mains should be easily accessed from water fountains or dispensers. These should preferably be located in circulation areas, as provision combined with toilet facilities is potentially unhygienic. For hygiene reasons, paper cups or similar should be provided. If positioned well, visual supervision should prevent vandalism.

STADTISCHE GESAMTSCHULE BARMEN, WUPPERTAL, GERMANY
A glazed three-storey 'street' runs the length of the building. As well as being the main circulation route, it provides an attractive place for informal work and recreation, full of plants and with views of ponds outside. The street also has environmental benefits as south-facing glazing contributes heating through passive solar energy. The plants provide shade and oxygen.

NIGHTINGALE NURSERY, HACKNEY, LONDON
The colourful butterfly image on these double doors is both welcoming and stimulating for the children.

GAINSBOROUGH ADVENTURE PLAYGROUND, LINCOLNSHIRE
Colour and texture can create an attractive area.

2B.4 FINISHES, FIXTURES AND LANDSCAPING

- Colour, texture and scent can help to create a stimulating environment.
- Good quality finishes and fixtures may cost more initially but will give better long term value for money.

Schools must be designed to be welcoming, stimulating places. It may be necessary to move away from the traditional institutional aesthetic, but this will benefit all users, including staff and pupils. Artists are sometimes included in a building project's design team, contributing in various ways, including artworks, colour schemes and landscaping design. The following ideas are worth considering when designing a school for the future:

- Variation in surface texture can help to minimise the sense of a large institution;
- Colour can be used to create an attractive and exciting place;
- Colour and surface finishes (internally and externally) can aid the visually impaired and elderly to orientate themselves (see Building Bulletin 94);
- Clear signing and 'indicators' should be included for the visually impaired;
- Interior planting can create a positive visual image and improve the air quality;

HAUTE VALLEE SCHOOL, JERSEY
On this secondary school, which was completed in 1998, a variety of finishes (brick, glass, render, cedar cladding) emphasises the differences between teaching blocks and suggests a village cluster of buildings which breaks down the building scale.

WESTBOROUGH PRIMARY SCHOOL, ESSEX
Children's designs on the tubes give a sense of ownership.

STADTISCHE GESAMTSCHULE BARMEN, GERMANY
Quality finishes can provide long term value for money.

- External finishes can be used to create interest and help environmental conditions (for example light coloured pavements will reflect light into ground floor rooms);
- Planting can provide shelter and shading for the external environment as well as benefiting the interior;
- Strongly scented plants can assist visually impaired people with orientation.

While some of these measures can add to the initial capital cost, they can provide long term value for money. Higher quality finishes, fittings and fixtures better serve the needs of the school and other users and can have a lower maintenance cost. Better quality furniture often lasts longer and good quality windows and doors can provide a more secure building envelope. Facilities that are of an overall higher standard can be good income earners.

There are many changes that cost very little but provide a more inclusive environment, such as choosing non-glare paint, using contrasting colours to pick out edges and door handles, or selecting wheelchair-friendly carpeting.

Well-planned and maintained grounds can do much to enhance even small school sites. Landscaping can also be used to enhance security, for example by dense planting or mounds (but the design should avoid creating hiding places).

External landscaped areas can also be a valuable part of the learning experience for pupils with special needs. For example strongly scented plants can stimulate the visually impaired, while calming areas can be created for those with emotional and behavioural difficulties. Refer to Building Bulletin 94, Inclusive School Design.

SOUTH CAMDEN COMMUNITY SCHOOL, CAMDEN, LONDON
A variety of finishes add character in this circulation area.

STEPHEN HAWKING SCHOOL, TOWER HAMLETS, LONDON
This special school for 70 pupils aged 2-11 opened in 1996. The interior of the building is full of light and colour.

WESTBOROUGH PRIMARY SCHOOL, WESTCLIFF-ON-SEA, ESSEX
Innovative designs such as these locker 'cages' can be attractive as well as functional.

YEWLANDS SCHOOL, SHEFFIELD
Narrow work surfaces may be used for informal access to computers.

2B.5 FURNITURE

- Higher quality furniture is expected in schools today.
- Furniture can help to make spaces more flexible.

The quality of school furniture is often below that in other community spaces and offices, yet people consider furniture a key aspect of a school's interior. This was demonstrated by the School I'd Like competition, in which pupils included comfortable seating and better height tables on their wish list for an ideal school. A school of the future accommodating a range of users should have something more attractive than standard school furniture, although it should be built for heavy use (see Furniture and Equipment in Schools: a Purchasing Guide). Ergonomics should be considered, especially as a greater range of people will be using the furniture. The needs of both adults and children should be considered.

Where PCs are used, specialist computer tables will be needed. This will not be the case for small portable equipment, although tables should be large enough to allow for a laptop to be used alongside paperwork. In informal work areas, possibly even in wide circulation areas, fairly narrow standing-height work surfaces may be appropriate, taking up a minimal amount of space. Where laptops are used in practical areas, space must be allowed to 'park' the equipment during practical activities. Furniture in dedicated ICT spaces will be more specialised, with adjustable chairs preferred to ensure a comfortable viewing height.

The choice of furniture can aid flexibility by making it easy to reconfigure spaces or create space within a space. Tables should be light enough to move around to suit different activities (although this must be balanced with

---

MODERN FOREIGN LANGUAGES ROOM ARRANGED FOR THREE DIFFERENT ACTIVITIES

1 **Pupils presenting to their peers who sit at tables facing forward.**

2 **Pupils working independently or in small groups.**

3 **Pupils talking to each other in the foreign language.**

Flexibility is helped by the fact that the furniture is easy to move and the amount of fixed furniture and equipment is minimised. This allows a variety of different layouts within the single room.

VICTORIA INFANTS SCHOOL, TIPTON, SANDWELL
The shared resource area includes library and food bays.
Activity areas are defined by furniture, much of it designed
specifically for the project.

the need for sturdiness in some practical
areas). Fixed furniture should be avoided
unless essential, as it restricts rearrangement.
Tables should as far as possible be useful
for a number of different activities. A table
in a food room, for example, can be put next
to fixed benches and used as an additional
practical work surface if it is the right
height. Trolleys help flexibility because
they can take resources to a space to
transform its function.

Adjustable tables and chairs may be
considered where there are likely to be large
variations in height of those using a space, e.g. if
adults are to use a primary group space. This
arrangement may be limited to one or two
spaces to reduce costs. An alternative to this is
to have an extra set of furniture for some
spaces, but this will require storage. Adjustable
furniture may be helpful for some special
needs pupils.

NEIGHBOURHOOD NURSERY COMPETITION WINNER, LONDON BOROUGH OF BEXLEY
Moveable pieces of furniture in this nursery design are conceived as theatrical
stage pieces. These 'city blocks' vary in size and shape and are designed to
work like Russian dolls, providing big blocks for adult assembly and smaller
blocks for children to handle. They pack away into colour co-ordinated
'docking zones'. These include fixed curved ramps on which children can run
which create a lively wall with pull-out pieces and personal storage. Nooks
left by the pull out objects can be used for activities like resting and reading.
The city blocks can be used together or individually to support role-playing
and other activities. Block types include 'wheelie classrooms' – integrated
table, chair and pencil case units – which stack to make a table and double as
a trolley on which the wheel hubs twist open to access storage chambers.
'Rubber roll out landscapes' are foam trees and plants which plug into rubber
sockets on a rubber play mat to create a tactile wobbly play space.

HEINAVAARA ELEMENTARY SCHOOL, FINLAND
Attractive but sturdy furniture helps
create a positive environment.

BARNHILL SCHOOL, HILLINGDON
The access needs of all users should be considered.

2C THOUGHTFUL PLANNING

Schools are always changing to facilitate new ways of learning and organisation. It is not possible therefore to create a plan that will work forever. There should be a clear masterplan, which provides a framework within which change can take place. This section looks at some of the key issues that should be considered when planning a school. At the end of the section a few generic plan types for both primary and secondary schools are illustrated. The characteristics of each are highlighted from which a number of useful lessons can be learnt. The sections are as follows:

2C.1   Planning the site
2C.2   Access and circulation
2C.3   Links and location
2C.4   Adaptability
2C.5   Plan types

2C.1 PLANNING THE SITE

- The site should be in the heart of the community, minimising transport costs.
- Take advantage, and consider the effect of buildings on the natural environment.

The location of the school is an important consideration from the point of view of both attracting customers and sustainability. The site should be in the heart of the community so minimising transport use, and allowing safe routes to school and access to public or school transport. School security is also important. For example, a school in a remote area is more vulnerable because it is not overlooked by neighbours. The presence or absence of utilities should be noted as well as the environmental cost of new provision.

One of the first issues to be discussed, once the site is chosen, is site access. Ease of access for a wider range of users will have to be balanced with the need for security. Will there be a secure boundary around the site with one controlled entry point or will there be public routes across the site, encouraging access and possibly helping supervision?

At this stage the site layout should be considered. Key issues include:

- Sustainability – minimising the impact on existing flora/fauna/trees and ground water and water courses;
- Building location – placing the buildings to draw in the community and providing good links to learning and recreation areas;
- Building orientation – taking account of the natural environment (daylight, sunlight, wind direction, noise and other such factors);

HAVERSTOCK SCHOOL, CAMDEN, LONDON
The proposed replacement plan for this 1200-place school situates it right on the street front with a bold façade making its presence felt in this street, a main route through the borough.

- Adaptability - the possibility of future expansion and the effect on external areas.

An inclusive school offering family and community services must consider the access needs of a range of users, including those with disabilities, the elderly and those with pushchairs. The site will have to account for those arriving by vehicle. There are likely to be more occasional visitors including support staff and community users. Consider:

- The possibility of additional car parking for visitors;
- Disabled car parking spaces near to entrances;
- Access routes for public transport or coaches especially in remote locations;
- Space for dropping off disabled users;
- Access to school, and – if separate – community entrances.

There should be easy access to school and community entrances for all users.

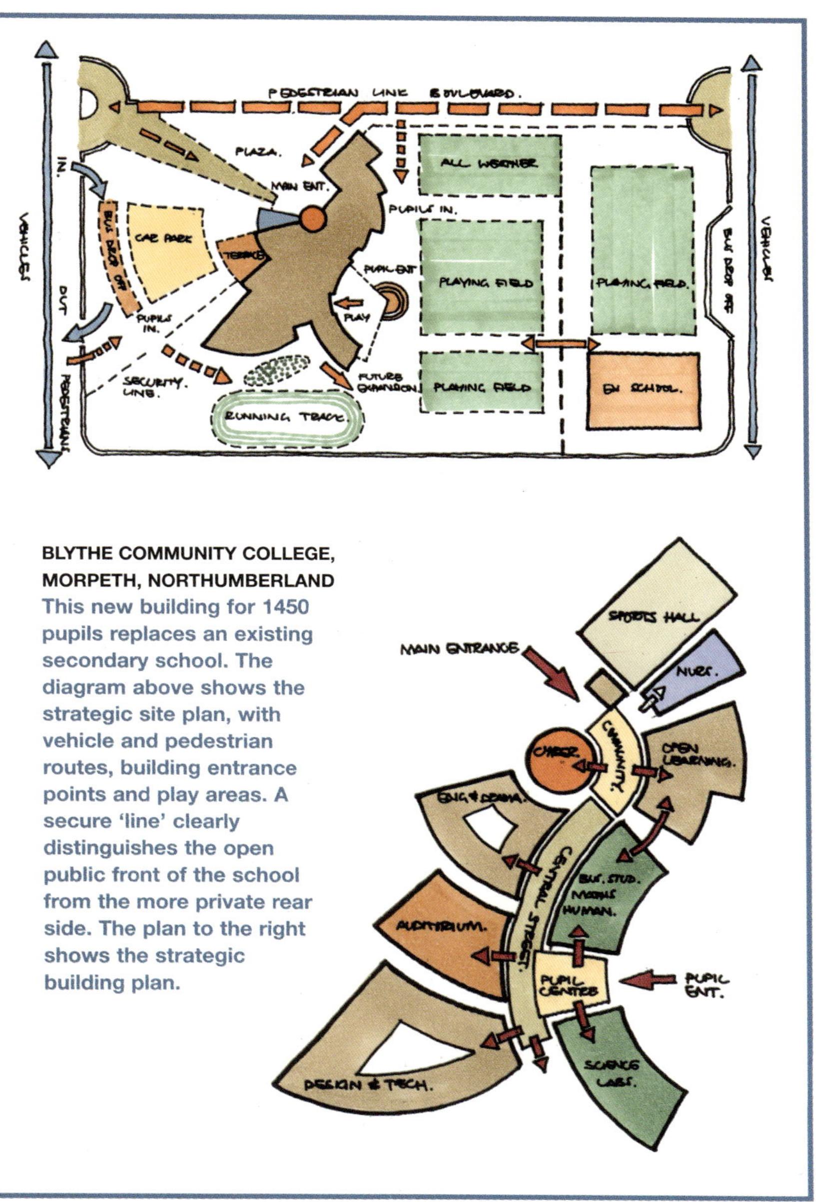

BLYTHE COMMUNITY COLLEGE, MORPETH, NORTHUMBERLAND
This new building for 1450 pupils replaces an existing secondary school. The diagram above shows the strategic site plan, with vehicle and pedestrian routes, building entrance points and play areas. A secure 'line' clearly distinguishes the open public front of the school from the more private rear side. The plan to the right shows the strategic building plan.

ALFRED SALTER SCHOOL, SOUTHWARK, LONDON
This wavy wall separates the more 'public' parts of the school from the 'private' areas (see plan on opposite page).

2C.2 ACCESS AND CIRCULATION

- Circulation routes should be clear to all (not just regular) users.
- Privacy may be desirable in some parts of the school.

The circulation pattern of a school is an important planning point that must be got right early in the design stage. There should be a clear circulation strategy covering all levels from access to the buildings to local circulation between spaces.

As there will be more people using schools in the future who are not familiar with the buildings, entrances should be clear and welcoming. This should be achieved through architecture, not just signage. School buildings and their surrounding environment should be physically accessible to all potential users (see Building Bulletins 91 and 94).

The number of entry points into the building will need to be considered, particularly in a large school. Will there be a single point of entry into the building(s) or will there be a number of entrances according to the nature of the user (e.g. pre-school, school pupils, business users and community users)? The former may be easier to secure but the latter may reduce congestion.

Circulation routes within the building(s) should be easy to follow, particularly to those parts of the school most likely to be used by those unfamiliar with the building, such as a performance space. Routes should be clear even without signs. Legible routes are especially

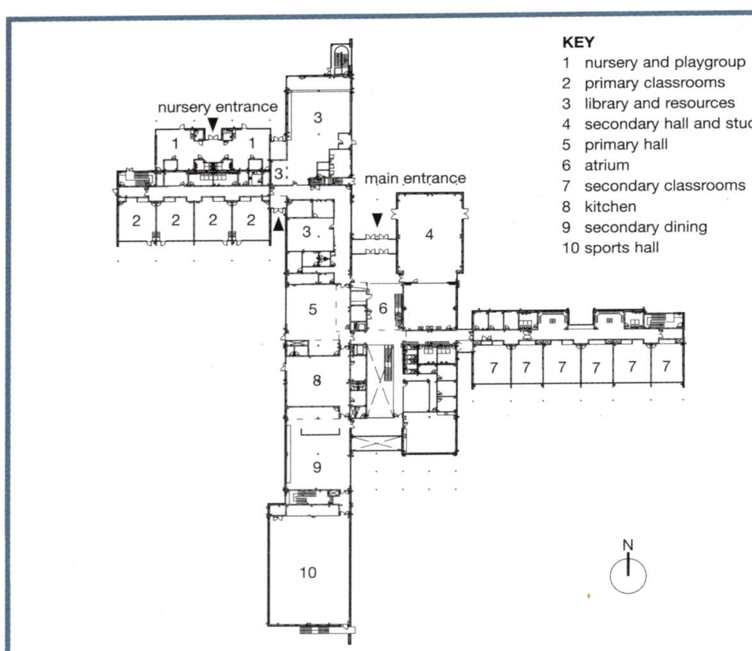

KEY
1. nursery and playgroup
2. primary classrooms
3. library and resources
4. secondary hall and studio
5. primary hall
6. atrium
7. secondary classrooms
8. kitchen
9. secondary dining
10. sports hall

CHAFFORD HUNDRED LEARNING CAMPUS, THURROCK, ESSEX

The ground floor plan for this all-age community school (also described in Section 1.3) is based on a cross-shape. A central spine houses all the large and specialist spaces (halls, library, sports, drama, dining, science design and technology, and art) which are most likely to be shared with the community.

The main entrance and another entrance from the car park lead to an atrium in the central spine. The nursery has a separate entrance. The primary classrooms and one wing of secondary classes are self contained and cannot be reached without passing through security doors.

The library is positioned to be accessible from the central circulation 'street' and directly from the outside when the rest of the school is shut. It has additional security cameras. An adjacent smaller-scale library is accessible from the primary wing for younger children. There is one kitchen serving primary and secondary halls.

GREAT BINFIELD, HAMPSHIRE
This new mainstream school (see the description in Section 2B.1) is planned with visually impaired children in mind. The route to the main entrance is made clear. Once inside, the reception desk is obviously positioned. The circulation plan is simple so that users can remember it easily and fragrant plants are used to orientate pupils.

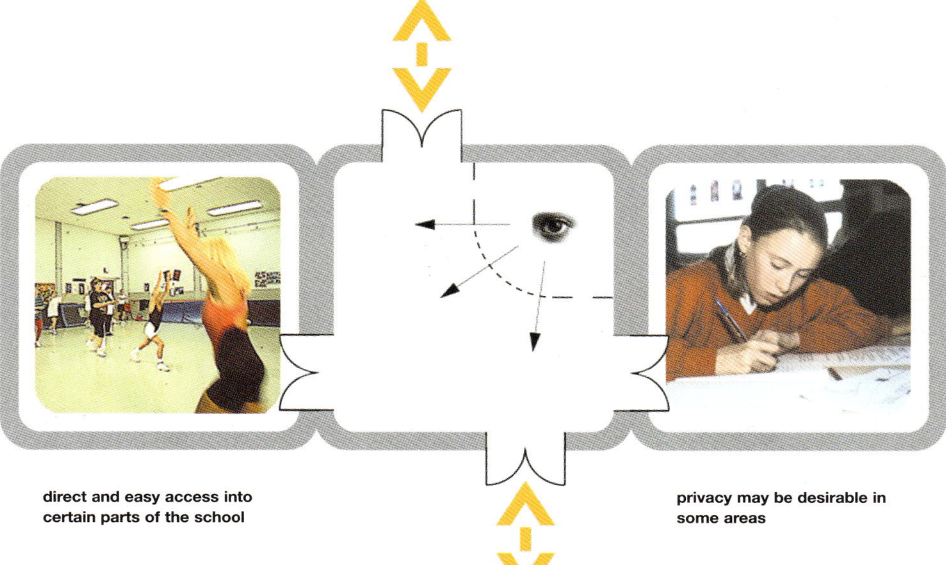

PLANNING FOR SECURITY
Openness needs to be balanced with security and privacy.

direct and easy access into certain parts of the school

privacy may be desirable in some areas

important to those who are visually impaired or those SEN pupils for whom research shows that predictability is important. Circulation should make efficient use of available area and where appropriate there should be overlap between circulation and social or study space.

Users should agree the extent to which areas of the school are open to all. Openness needs to be balanced against security, particularly if there are 0-5 year-olds on site (although security concerns should not affect the function of the school). The school may want to limit the number of people passing certain rooms at various times during the day, particularly during examination times. Routes can be designed to ensure some private areas for school pupils such as spaces used for examinations or consultation rooms. It may be useful to group spaces together that are most often used after school hours to allow zoning of services and better security.

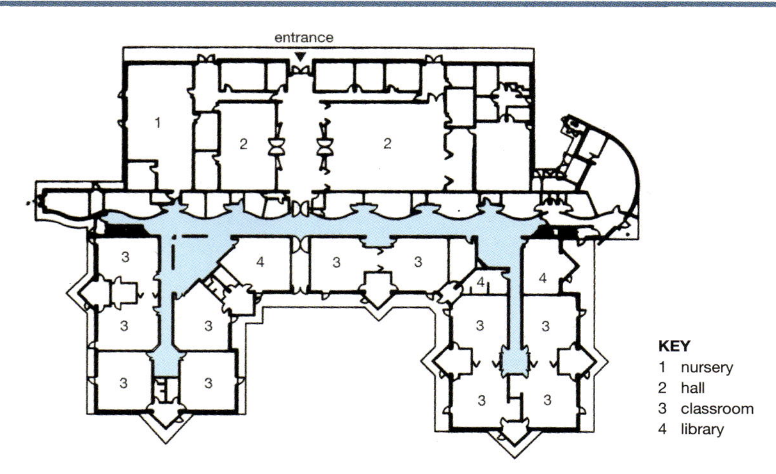

ALFRED SALTER PRIMARY SCHOOL, SOUTHWARK, LONDON
The plan is arranged with entrance, offices, hall and nursery on one side of a spine wall and classrooms on the other. The nursery and community spaces can therefore be reached without going into the main part of the school. Classrooms are in two wings: infants and juniors. The configuration allows more classrooms to be added in the future.

TANBRIDGE HOUSE SCHOOL, HORSHAM, WEST SUSSEX
All design and technology spaces are linked together in a block with shared resource and display areas.

2C.3 LINKS AND LOCATION

■ Spaces shared by all users should be centrally located.
■ Links between activities should be understood.

It is essential to understand the workings of a school in order to plan it successfully. It is important to understand when and by whom spaces are used in order to decide on their location. It is also valuable to know the relationship between activities so that spaces can be usefully grouped together. For example, a space that is used by all may be best located at the heart of the school and easily accessible from the entrance. Some subject areas can be usefully grouped together.

The following summarises the key points to consider about the location of spaces within the school plan.

● The central library/ICT resource area and other main school facilities should be easily accessible to all and visible to those entering the school as visitors.
● The cafeteria, whether shared between the school and community, or separate, should be located for easy access by all users.
● The kitchen should link to all refreshment facilities.
● Toilets should be conveniently located and easy to supervise. A disabled toilet in each block is advisable. At primary level it is useful to have access from the playground.

● SEN and learning support spaces need to feel private and quiet but not isolated from the rest of the school.
● In secondary schools, small general resource areas can be anywhere in the school but specialist resource areas are best located close to related group spaces.
● Noisy spaces (for example, kitchens) are best located away from noise sensitive spaces such as music rooms.

The key points about links between activities (and therefore spaces) are listed below.
● Spaces that are likely to share resources and equipment should be grouped together (for example art and textiles spaces in secondary).
● The introduction of the foundation stage has strengthened links between nursery and reception areas.
● Most group spaces will require easy access to supporting spaces (for example, store rooms, technicians' rooms or resource areas).
● Learning support staff tend to share practice and communicate more effectively when they are situated in proximity to each other. It may therefore be advisable to group together spaces such as those for special educational needs and learning support. However, this should be balanced with the need to have multi-functional spaces for greater flexibility.

For further guidance on planning subject-specific spaces see Building Bulletins 80, 81, 86, 89 and 92.

DIAGRAMMATIC PLAN SHOWING KEY PLANNING POINTS

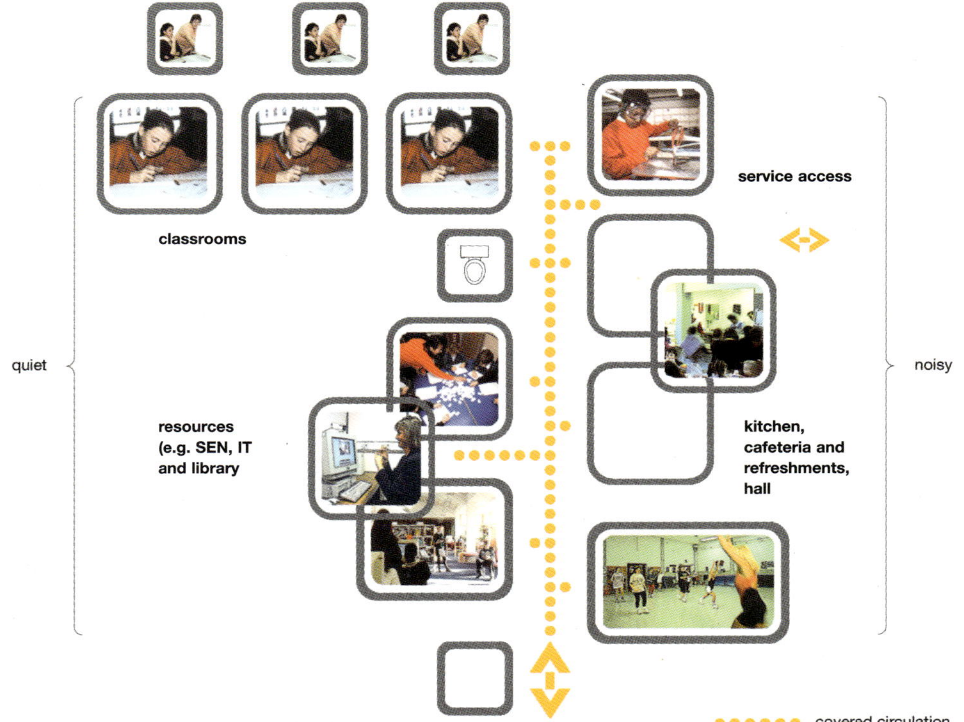

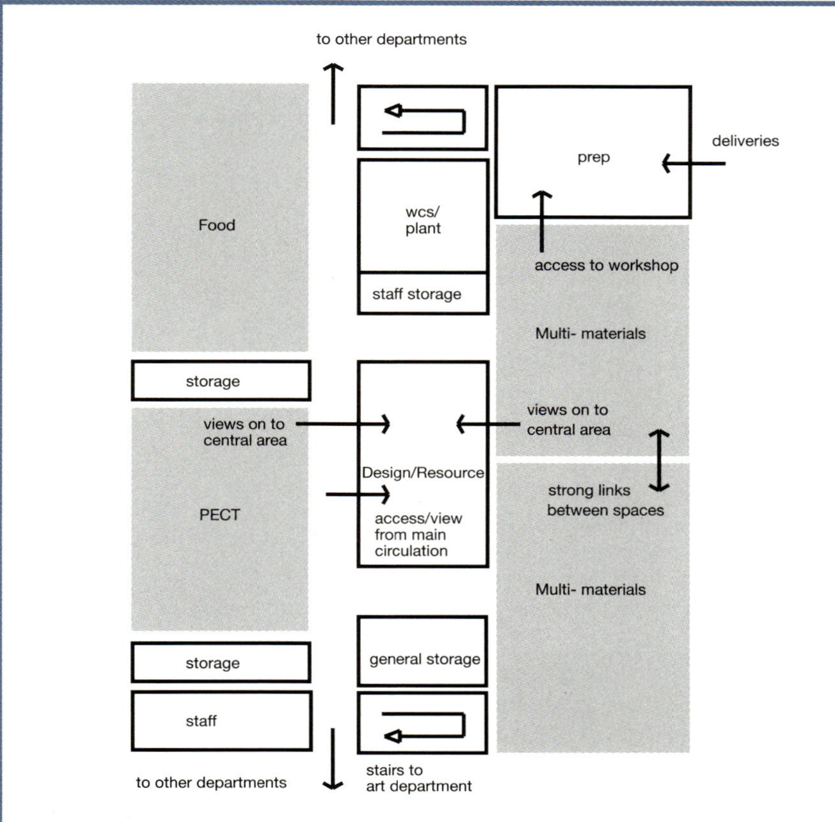

DESIGN AND TECHNOLOGY AREA LINKS
Key links should be created for the space to function fully: access to shared resource areas from specialist areas; access to storage from learning base; access to preparation rooms from teaching spaces and external services areas (for deliveries); visual links between learning spaces and circulation and shared areas; central staff bases in heart of the suite, with access from main circulation; and links to other activities such as claywork or textiles in art.

BARNHILL SCHOOL, HILLINGDON
Shared spaces should be centrally located.

KEY
1 classroom
2 hall
3 junior dining/studio
4 entrance foyer
5 kitchen
6 library
7 nursery
8 community room
9 quiet area
10 office
11 studio/music
12 plant
13 w.c.
14 store

VICTORIA INFANTS SCHOOL, SANDWELL

This school provides for 270 infants, and also has a 45-place nursery and community facilities. Some spaces are shared with the adjacent junior school, the kitchen serves both schools. The plan affects the range of activities accommodated. At one end of the linear plan is the infants' entrance and at the other (close to the junior school) is a cluster of shared facilities (hall, studios and kitchen).

Close to the road is a multi-agency centre, which supplies advice and social services to parents, and encourages them to participate in the life of the school. Next to it is the nursery, linked to the reception classes for the youngest infants. Classrooms curve round to the north, benefiting from the morning sun, with views into, and access to, the heart of the site. All the classes open into an internal 'street', which provides space for shared libraries, cookery, science and technology.

DJANOGLY CITY TECHNOLOGY COLLEGE, NOTTINGHAM
The school is planned around a grid. The structure allows a maximum room depth in classroom blocks of 9m with a shallower alternative of 7.2m. This limits the range of rooms to allow easy adaptations. Staircases and toilet blocks are located to have a minimum effect on partition relocation. Ceiling heights of 2.7m suit general and practical spaces.

JERSEY COLLEGE FOR GIRLS AND VICTORIA COLLEGE
School buildings often have a long life and spaces may have to serve many functions.

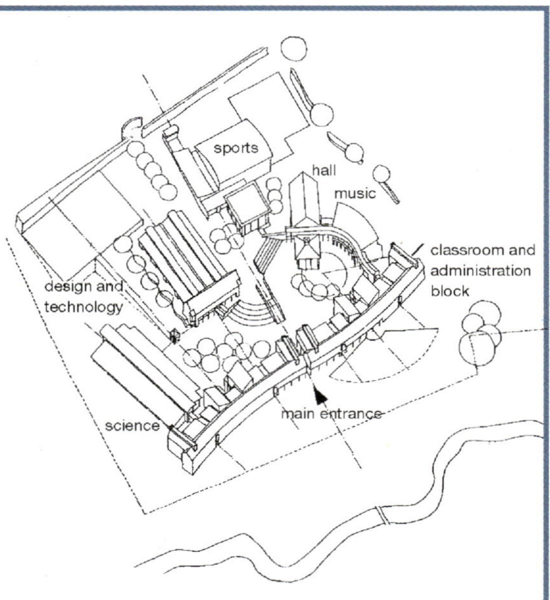

TANBRIDGE HOUSE SCHOOL, HORSHAM WEST SUSSEX
Designed as a 1200-place school with the possibility of expansion to 1500. Sports spaces are designed for 1500. All classroom blocks are simple linear plans designed to extend. The hall has an end wall that can be removed for expansion. The architects had to consider the location on the site and a structure that would allow expansion.

2C.4 ADAPTABILITY

- Expansion and adaptation should always be allowed for.
- The location of services and structure should not restrict adaptation.

Schools buildings are not static; they adapt over time to meet changing needs. Adaptability should therefore be considered at the design stage. A number of unpredictable changes can lead to the need for adaptation or expansion:

- Range of users (e.g. more SEN pupils);
- Numbers of users (e.g. due to population fluctuations);
- Type or balance of activities (e.g. due to curriculum developments, or an increased range of family and community provision);
- Organisational structure (e.g. different group sizes).

A good model of adaptability is a speculative office building, which is basically a shell with services that are expensive to move (lift, stairs, toilets etc) concentrated in a core. This format is not, however, wholly applicable to schools where the frequency of adaptation doesn't justify the expense of office-standard relocatable partitions. The partitions of an office building may be moved as often as every two years but the partitions in a school are more likely to be moved every 5-10 years.

The need to consider expansion when preparing the site plan is examined in section 2C.1. The building form should also be considered — some buildings, for example simple linear plans, are easier to adapt than others. 'Statement' buildings and more idiosyncratic buildings can be difficult to extend.

ALFRED SALTER SCHOOL, SOUTHWARK, LONDON This primary school has been designed to allow for expansion. At the end of each classroom-wing, arm extensions can be added, as seen here. Core facilities such as the hall are sized for more pupils (420) than the school's initial intake (see plan in Section 2C.2).

When planning the location of spaces within the school buildings it is worth considering which spaces are most likely to change. Broadly speaking there are three types of space:

- Those that are unlikely to expand (e.g. the reception area and head's room);
- Those that are likely to grow to suit extra numbers (e.g. the hall or staff room) although this will depend on frequency of use;
- Those that will be replicated (e.g. classrooms).

The size and shape of individual spaces may also reduce the need for adaptations. Limiting the depth of spaces to one or two dimensions could make adaptation simpler, for example. Standard ceiling heights (as far as possible) makes changes in room size more straightforward.

The location of services and major structural elements will also have an effect on adaptability. This includes main service risers, staircases, any lifts and plant rooms. If drainage runs are kept to the perimeter of buildings, they can remain undisturbed if partitions are moved about. Heavily serviced spaces should be positioned to allow future adaptations to rooms and functions.

There are times when temporary accommodation is needed to cope with fluctuations in pupil numbers. Temporary buildings can be useful as a short-term measure, but they should not be seen as a cheap alternative to permanent buildings. Their construction tends to have inherent disadvantages such as poor environmental conditions, lack of insulation, poor acoustics and lack of security.

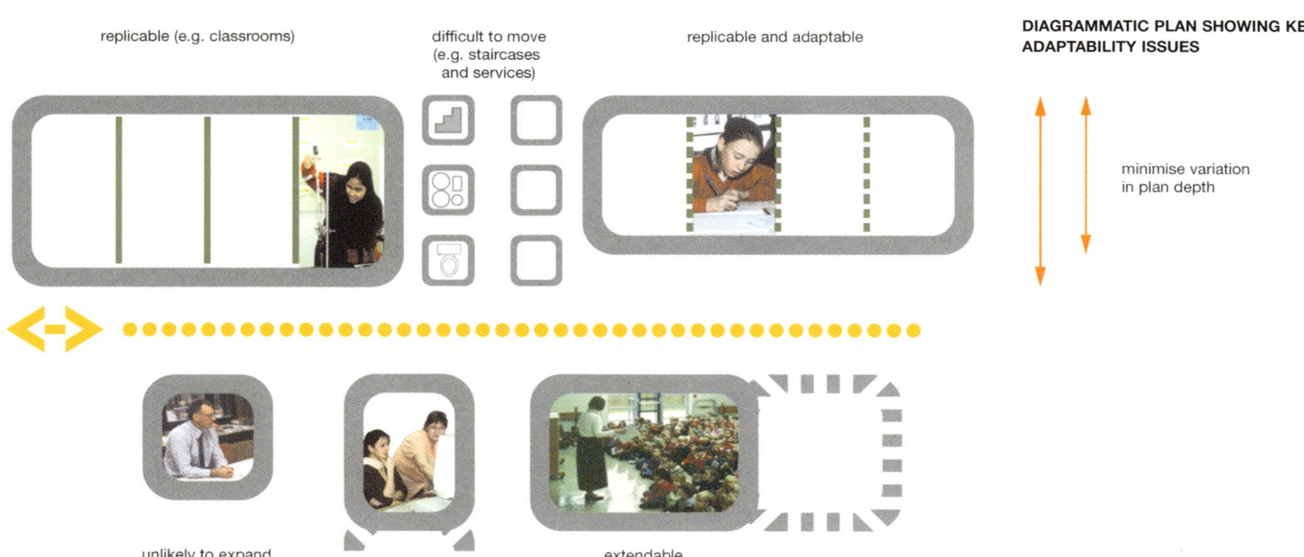

JIM LOWE

PERTHCELYN COMMUNITY PRIMARY SCHOOL, SOUTH WALES
The linear plan of this school is used flexibly over two storeys on this steeply sloping site. The storeys are vertically linked to create a shared heart to the school.

2C.5 PLAN TYPES

Many school plans are derived from the same generic plan type. Each has particular characteristics. For example, linked pavilions break down the scale in a large secondary school, but can be inflexible and difficult to extend because of the finite forms. Deep plans are efficient and environmentally good for heat retention but can cause ventilation problems (especially if courtyards are later filled in). A single building is easier to manage than several, and complex forms with many hidden recesses can increase security risk.

This page and the next show three secondary school plans: street, campus and linked pavilions. The characteristics of each are listed alongside. Following that are three typical primary school plan types: pavilion, linear and deep linear.

▶ **SECONDARY SCHOOL: STREET PLAN**
The plan is based on a street grid with a main 'street' two or three storeys high forming the main circulation spine and focus for school life. The main street may be the most public route. Secondary circulation routes run at right angles to the street, giving access to different faculties. Characteristics include:

- **The street provides a focus to the school and acts as an internal recreation space;**
- **Classrooms receive borrowed light from the street;**
- **The building is compact, reducing cost and heat loss;**
- **Courtyards are required to bring daylight to the deep plan;**
- **Areas away from the spine are fairly easy to adapt;**
- **Access to individual faculties can be restricted, if desired.**

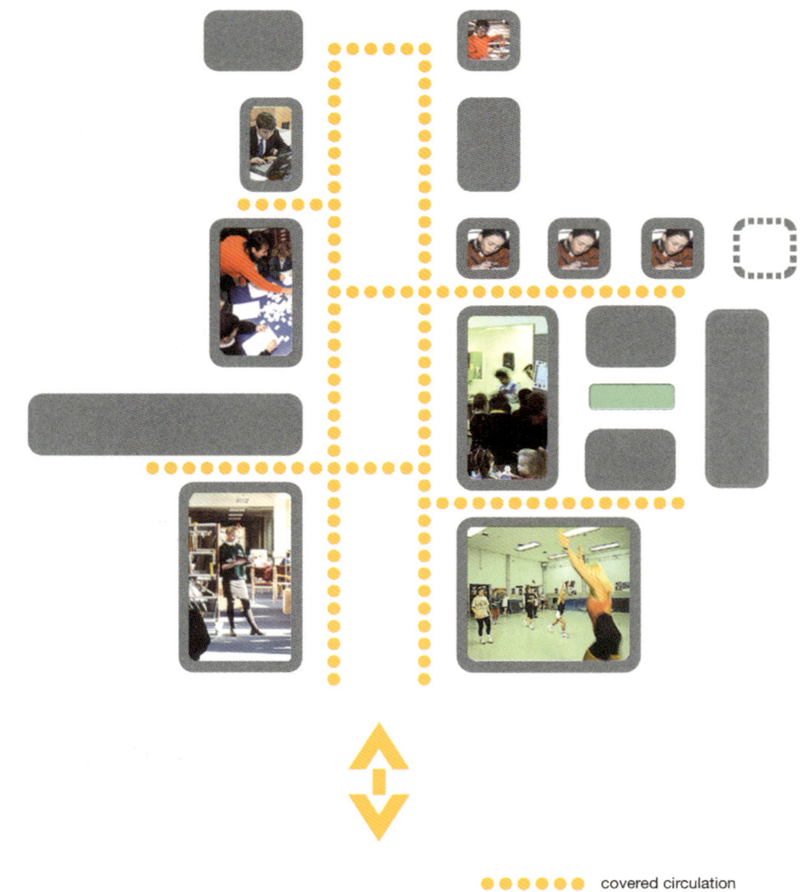

◄ **SECONDARY SCHOOL: CAMPUS PLAN**

Unlike the other plans some circulation is external. The school, is seen as a series of distinct blocks, grouped together in a 'village'. Characteristics include:

- Each block can be different in scale and form to suit the activities it encloses;
- Blocks can use different materials, giving variety and interest to the site;
- The school can be easily adapted and extended as blocks are unattached. New blocks can also be added to the cluster;
- Pupils have to move outside between blocks;
- Spaces between blocks can be varied in shape and scale;
- Good ventilation is easily achieved but heat loss may be an issue.

●●●●●● external circulation

sheltered outdoor space

► **SECONDARY SCHOOL: LINKED PAVILIONS**

The plan is made up from a number of linked blocks. Classroom blocks are similar in form, group spaces surrounding a double-height central space. Large spaces form a separate block. Characteristics include:

- Each block can reflect a faculty in both its form and display (for example a humanities or science block);
- The central space can form a shared resource area, easily accessed by surrounding spaces;
- Each block can also act as a year or house base with pupils gathering in the central area;
- A pavilion can be opened separately for out of hours use;
- Sheltered courtyards can be created between pavilions;
- The blocks are closed in form and not easy to extend;
- Circulation through pavilions may be complex.

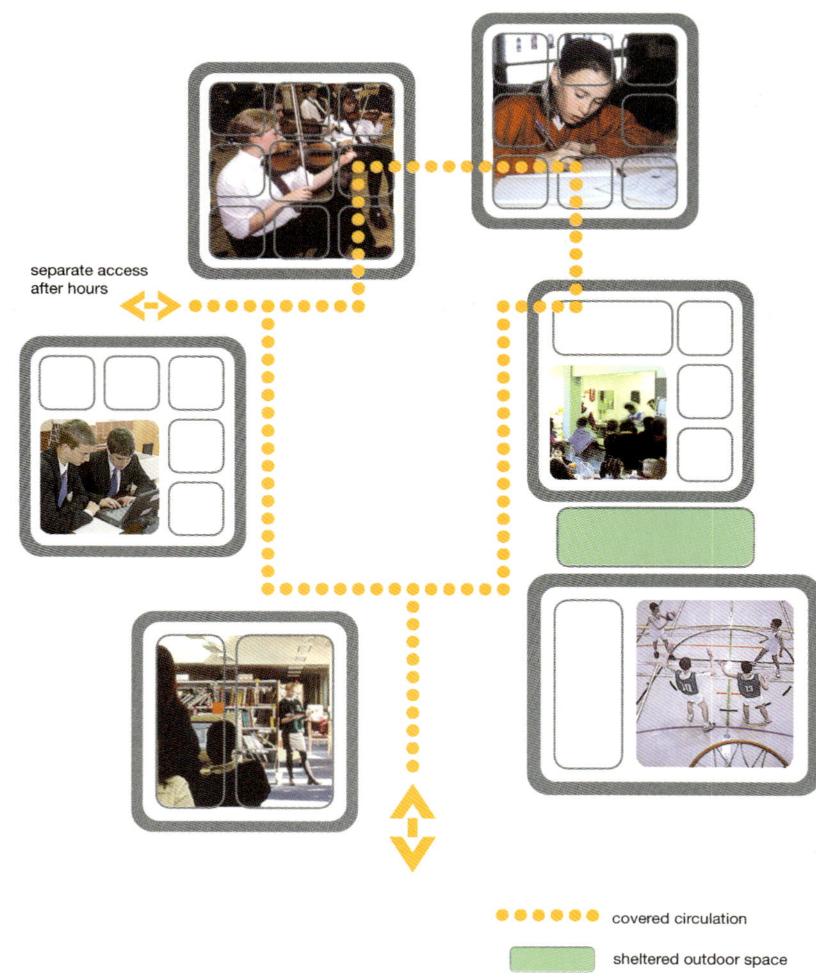

●●●●●● covered circulation

sheltered outdoor space

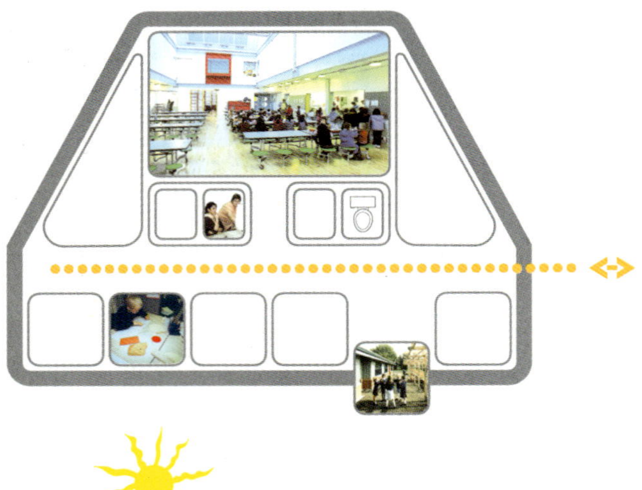

◄ PRIMARY SCHOOL: PAVILION PLAN

A deep plan with classrooms and resource areas each side of a circulation route with the hall positioned centrally.
Characteristics (some shared with linear plan, below) include:

- All classrooms face roughly the same direction, preferably south-ish;
- Easy classroom access to local resource areas, toilets and cloakrooms;
- Direct pupil (and parent) access from playground to classrooms at each end of the day;
- Centrally positioned hall easily reached from all classrooms;
- Compact plan;
- Some exclusively internal spaces due to the deep plan;
- Extension may be less straightforward than with the other plans.

●●●●●● covered circulation

► PRIMARY SCHOOL: LINEAR PLAN

Classrooms are on one side of a circulation route with support spaces on the other. Hall and entrance are usually at one end of the classroom run. Characteristics include:

- All classrooms can have favourable orientation;
- A lower roof over smaller support rooms allows clerestory lighting and ventilation to back of classrooms;
- Easy classroom access to local resource areas, toilets and cloakrooms;
- Classrooms easily added if needed;
- Isolation of most used community spaces (e.g. hall) possible;
- Direct access to classrooms from playground at each end of the day;
- Building shape may result in long distances between classrooms and shared spaces such as hall.

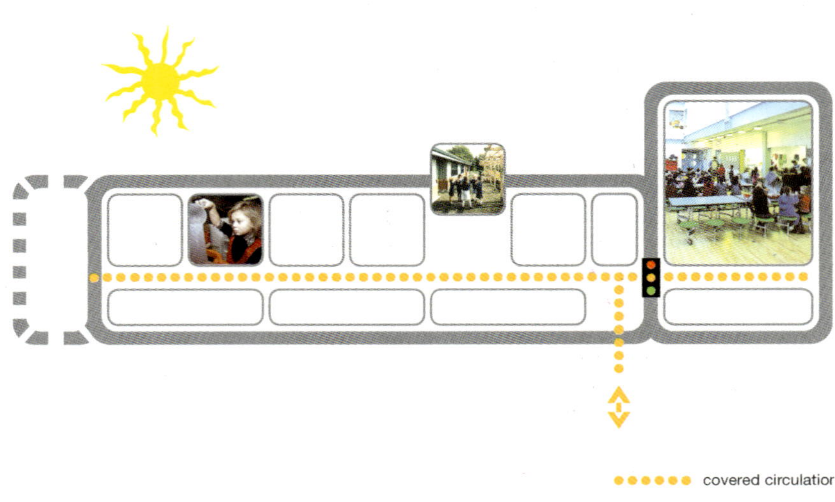

●●●●●● covered circulation

●● restricted access

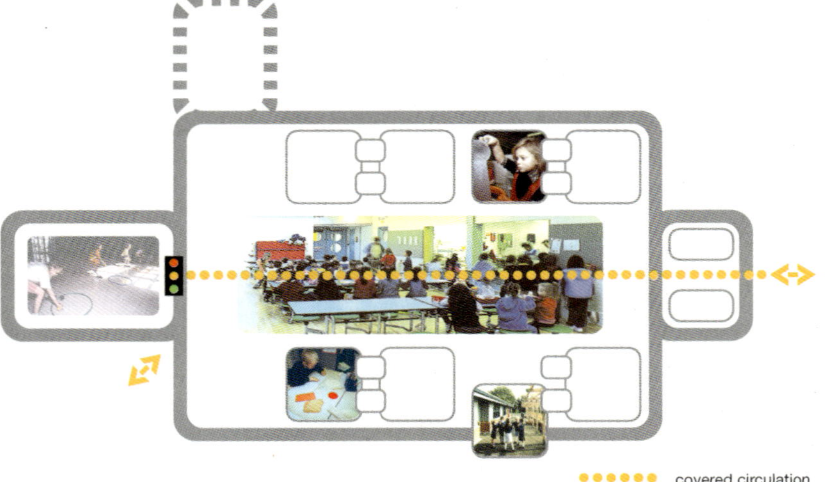

●●●●●● covered circulation

●● restricted access

◄ PRIMARY SCHOOL: DEEP LINEAR PLAN

Classroom bases are on two sides of a shared circulation/ resource area; hall and entrance at one end of the block. Characteristics include:

- Easy classroom access to resource areas;
- Blurring of boundary between base and open areas;
- Direct pupil and parent access to classrooms;
- Wide central area can house varying group sizes;
- Isolation of community spaces as linear plan;
- Compact with less external wall to floor area than linear plan;
- One row of classrooms may have less favourable orientation;
- Getting daylight and ventilation to rear of classrooms may be more difficult;
- No external view from central areas.

2D SUSTAINABLE SCHOOL

Buildings have a major impact on the environment, not just in terms of materials used in construction, but also due to energy usage during their lifetime. As buildings last a long time it is important they are of a sustainable design. Sustainability is both an environmental and social aim, and should be considered throughout the building process. The complete building can be a lesson in sustainability for the building's users – sustainability is now part of the National Curriculum – and the public. The section is split into two:

2D.1   General approach
2D.2   Energy efficiency

NOTLEY GREEN PRIMARY, BRAINTREE, ESSEX
Notley Green was designed as a flagship sustainable school and its grass roof acts as a dramatic symbol of its intention.

2D.1 GENERAL APPROACH

- A long term view is needed to take advantage of sustainable design solutions.
- Sustainability should inform the whole building process.

Sustainability should be considered at all stages of the building process, starting with the design concept, the site analysis and the location of the building in the environment. The detailed design and specification of the building should ensure that both short and long-term impacts on the environment are kept to a minimum.

Sustainability issues should be evaluated alongside other issues when building budgets are being set. Some sustainable design solutions may appear expensive but a long term view must be taken. The level of initial capital investment should be balanced against a lifecycle cost analysis for each element of the building. Such methods allow the choice of materials and construction techniques that might otherwise have initially been disregarded on cost grounds.

The Government has set out its aims in the

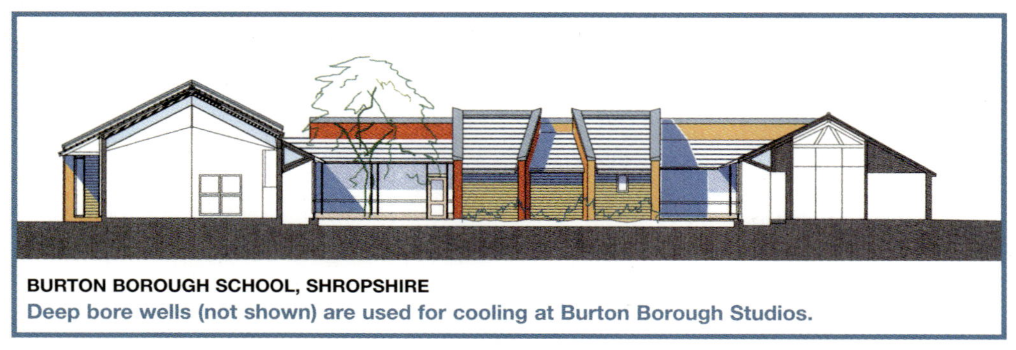

BURTON BOROUGH SCHOOL, SHROPSHIRE
Deep bore wells (not shown) are used for cooling at Burton Borough Studios.

On this school in the Netherlands photovoltaic cells generate some of the energy requirements.

LATYMER UPPER SCHOOL ARTS CENTRE AND THEATRE, HAMMERSMITH, LONDON
Sustainability means working with the existing environment, for example using elements such as the tree shown here to good advantage.

'Satisfying basic human needs; privileging quality of life over material standards of living; minimising resource use, waste, and pollution; taking a lifecycle approach; and acting with concern for future generations.'
Defining Sustainability, Oslo Symposium (1994)

document Sustainable Development Strategy (1999). Many Local Authorities have developed Local Agenda 21 strategies on sustainable development in their areas. Building Bulletin 83, Schools Environment Assessment Method (SEAM), provides a framework for designing a sustainable school, and allows schools to carry out a self assessment of how environmentally-friendly their school, or school design, is.

Sustainability impacts on many aspects of a schools design. The main issues to consider are:

- Selection of site to minimise transport use;
- Orientation of the building to maximise daylight, reduce noise disturbance, etc;
- Use of local and recycled materials;
- Use of timber from sustainable sources;
- Minimisation of construction waste;
- Design for low maintenance.

The most important aspect of sustainability is to design for low energy usage. This not only limits use of fossil fuel but also reduces CO_2 emissions.

2D.2 ENERGY EFFICIENCY

- Energy conservation should be the keystone for the design of school buildings.
- Good housekeeping can reduce energy usage by 20%.

Once complete, buildings account for 50% of the UK's energy consumption. There is a long way to go in improving the energy efficiency of our buildings, which rarely reach the level of energy efficiency commonly found in Germany or Scandinavia. Energy conservation should be the keystone for the design of school buildings, especially as energy costs are increasing.

Some renewable energy sources are economic and well tried. Unfortunately, at present, many renewable energy sources like photovoltaic (solar power) cells, and wind-generators are only just economic but this

MILLENNIUM PRIMARY SCHOOL, GREENWICH, LONDON
Sustainability is at the heart of this school's environmental design. Tempered air is passed through the hollow core of the pre-cast concrete floor slabs using the Thermodeck system to exploit the thermal storage capacity of the building fabric, enabling the building to moderate its own internal climate, so occupied areas receive 100% fresh air, with free night-time cooling. The boiler plant is a fraction of normal size due to high level insulation and efficient heat reclamation of both casual and solar heat gains. Advanced modelling techniques were employed to optimise daylighting levels in the classrooms through the use of light (and ventilation) wells at the rear. Presence-detecting, energy-efficient electric lighting has been used throughout.

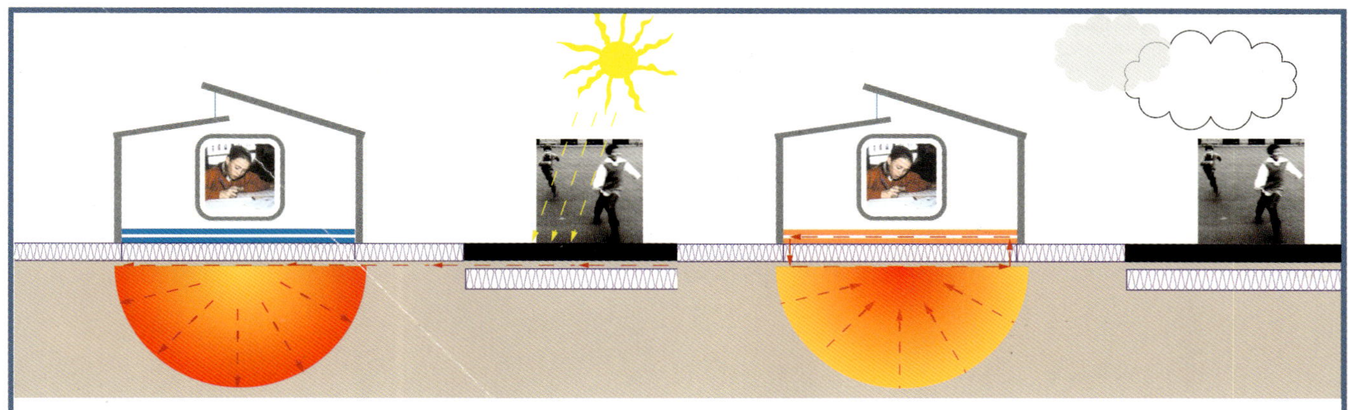

NEIGHBOURHOOD NURSERY, LONDON BOROUGH OF BEXLEY, COMPETITION WINNER
One of the innovative proposals for this neighbourhood nursery is to take advantage of the area of tarmac adjacent to the building to provide a large solar collector. The earth beneath the building will be used as a store and a water-glycol mixture will circulate in coils in these and floor heating coils to provide underfloor heating using summer collected solar heat.

could change very quickly as markets develop and capital costs come down. They can be considered as pilots, demonstration projects or in special circumstances.

The key features of an energy efficient design include:

- High levels of insulation;
- Good use of daylight and natural ventilation;
- High thermal mass (in the walls and ceilings) to avoid temperature fluctuations;
- Good temperature control and lighting control systems.

From April 2001, the Climate Change Levy started applying to energy use in schools, adding roughly 10% to school fuel bills. Gas prices are also rising sharply, so it is important that schools are energy efficient and that the users, including members of the community, learn to use the building and its energy controls properly. It has been estimated that simple good housekeeping measures can reduce energy usage by 20%.

Benchmarking programmes are available to enable schools to compare their energy and water consumption with other schools (for more information see www.watermark.gov.uk).

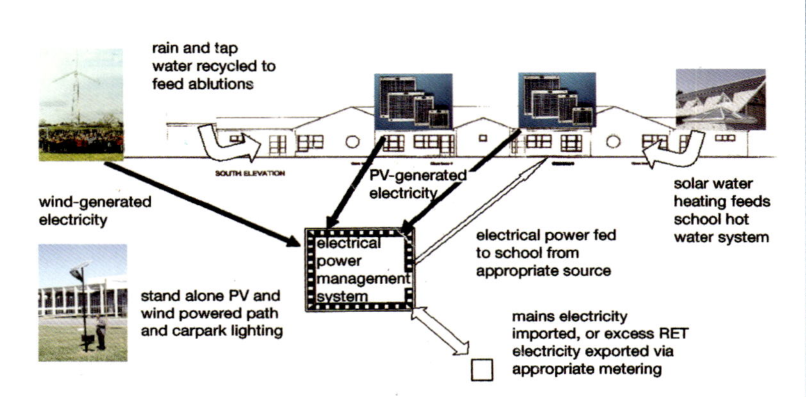

CROMWELL PARK PRIMARY SCHOOL, HUNTINGDON, CAMBRIDGESHIRE
This primary school in Huntingdon, Cambridgeshire, due to open in September 2002, is a Renewable Energy Technology (RET) project. It is designed to combine education about sustainability (as in the National Curriculum) and a reduction in energy consumption as a beacon of best practice. Proposals include a grey-water system to recycle rainwater and used tap water; photovoltaic panels; a wind turbine; and a solar water-heating system. The aim is to reduce energy bills, partly by exporting power to the national grid. Photovoltaic panels will power a number of the school's computers. An interactive display linking the weather conditions with the energy production from the solar and wind technologies around the school will teach children about sustainability.

WEOBLEY PRIMARY SCHOOL, HEREFORD, HEREFORDSHIRE
Weobley Primary School is the first UK school to be fuelled from burning locally-produced wood chips. As well as heating the 180-pupil primary school and the 30-pupil nursery school, the wood chips heat the older, adjacent secondary school.

Other sustainability features include:
- Making use of solar gain for lighting and heating;
- Use of natural materials, including a timber structure;
- Installation of user-friendly environmental controls, for heating and lighting, in the classrooms.

The design was completed in partnership with the end users, and it will be monitored in order to review its performance.

Left to right: Wonelly Secondary School, Southwark, London; Merryfield Nursery, Southwark, London. Opposite page: Notley Green Primary, Braintree, Essex.

3 THE BUILDING PROCESS

Part 3 looks at the building process and considers the issues that are critical to securing facilities that are fit for their purpose, well designed and provide value for money – now and in the foreseeable future.

Consultation and co-operation are key factors in achieving these objectives. This is true for all stages of the process, for example:

- Users should be consulted throughout the project;
- The brief should be developed jointly by all interested parties;
- All parties should work as a team towards a common goal.

The success of a school building project also depends on time and effort spent on investigation and analysis in the early stages of its development. The key issues are:

- Careful assessment of need;
- Consideration of a number of design options;
- Cost planning;
- Programming.

A 'design champion' in the Local Authority can help encourage design quality in schools' building projects. After the project is over, post-project evaluation is important in order to inform the development of future projects.

Further information on the above issues is set out in Sections 3.2 to 3.8. These sections are organised to broadly follow the main stages in the development of a building project. Section 3.1 outlines two recent initiatives, Asset Management Planning and Rethinking Construction, which set the context for school building projects now and in the future.

3.1   Setting the context
3.2   Consultation
3.3   Brief or output specification
3.4   Feasibility studies and option appraisals
3.5   Cost planning
3.6   Building procurement
3.7   Programming
3.8   Evaluation

TIM SOAR

KINGSWOOD SCHOOL, CANTERBURY, ENTRY INTO RIBA SUSTAINABLE SCHOOLS COMPETITION
Every project should be seen as part of long term plans for the school.

CHRIST CHURCH CE PRIMARY SCHOOL, KENSINGTON AND CHELSEA, LONDON
Consultation may involve getting clients and users (in this case children) to do their own designs.

3.1 SETTING THE CONTEXT

Two key initiatives, Asset Management Planning and Rethinking Construction, are having a significant effect on the management of the school building stock and on the way individual building projects are carried out. These developments are outlined below.

Asset Management Planning

All LEAs, in consultation with their schools, are developing asset management plans (AMPs). These plans provide a rigorous management framework within which the investment needs of schools across an area can be prioritised on an open, transparent and consultative basis and set out the necessary programmes of work needed to tackle the priorities identified.

Sound asset management planning should enable the increasingly large amounts of money becoming available for school buildings to be directed most effectively to where they can have the greatest impact on raising standards. In support of good asset management planning, the DfES would expect LEAs and schools to adopt, as appropriate, the processes and practices described in this section (for further information and assistance on AMPs see the DfES AMP web page at www.teachernet.gov.uk/sbamps).

Rethinking Construction

Sir John Egan's report, Rethinking Construction, looked at ways of improving the efficiency and quality of delivery of the UK construction industry. The report identified five key drivers for change: committed leadership; a focus on the customer; an integrated procurement process; a quality driven agenda; and commitment to people.

It was recognised that the construction industry needs to become less confrontational, more innovative and deliver improvement in performance. It also recommended targets for reductions in construction cost, time and defects.

The government is encouraging all public sector clients, including schools and LEAs, to apply the Rethinking Construction principles to their building projects. Among other things this approach can deliver:

- Savings in capital and revenue expenditure;
- Improved predictability in construction time and cost;
- Reduced defects;
- Reduced accidents;
- Increased customer satisfaction;
- Better whole life value.

Information on how to apply the above principles to projects can be obtained from the following bodies, which have been set up by the government to promote Rethinking Construction:

- Movement for Innovation (M4I) (www.m4i.org.uk).
- Local Government Task Force (www.lgtf.org.uk).

**WESTBOROUGH PRIMARY SCHOOL,
WESTCLIFF-ON-SEA, ESSEX**
Working together to think through design ideas can be a
valuable learning experience.

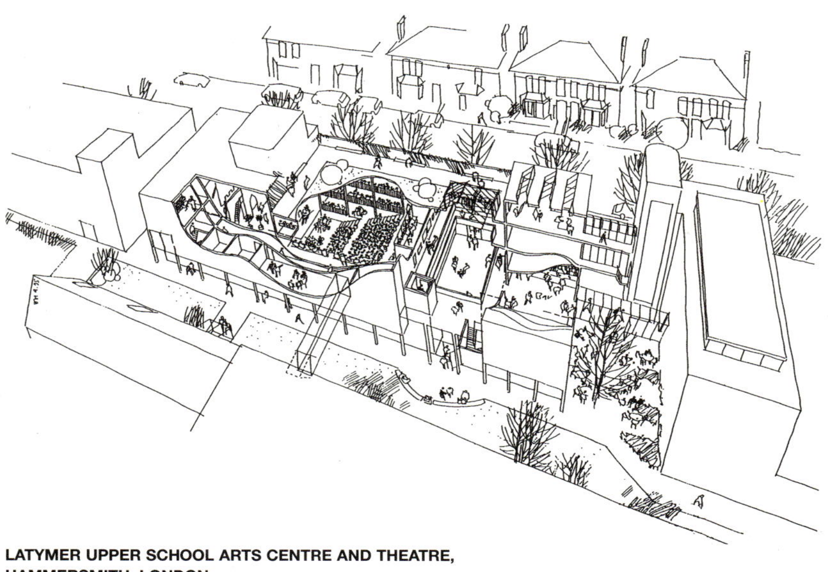

**LATYMER UPPER SCHOOL ARTS CENTRE AND THEATRE,
HAMMERSMITH, LONDON**
Slotting new facilities onto a site can be an opportunity to
involve the local community and other nearby schools.
Consultation can help ensure local needs are met.

3.2 CONSULTATION

The Rethinking Construction initiative
encourages a focus on the customer as a key
player in the success of a building project. It is
very important that right from the beginning of
a school building project there is proper
consultation with the staff and pupils of the
school and the wider community. The school
and its community must decide what they
need and want both for the immediate and
longer term future.

School consultation should involve both staff
and pupils. The Guardian newspaper's School
I'd Like competition attracted over 15,000
entries from pupils all over the country. The
findings and the winning entries were published
in the Guardian of 5th June 2001. Some of the
most popular things that pupils wanted were:

- 'Home-from-home' environment;
- Good furniture;
- Safe schools;
- Drinking water easily available;
- Better toilets;
- Quiet study rooms, 'chill-out' rooms;
- Lockers;
- Exciting ways of learning.

All potential users in the community should be
consulted in order to assess local and individual
needs as it may be possible to include facilities
that the community lacks, such as a nursery,
library, or sports hall, in the school building
project.

This approach will help to encourage
greater use of the building, develop trust
between all parties and add to the feeling of
community and ownership.

Other local schools, both primary and
secondary, that are likely to be affected
because their pupils might use the school,
should also be consulted.

SCHOOL WORKS PROJECT
**This initiative uses
participatory techniques at
the early stage of a project.
At Kingsdale School,
Southwark, all staff, pupils
and the local community
took part in workshops,
using creative techniques
from drama to art to assess
how they felt about the
existing buildings. School
Works, in collaboration with
Kingsdale School, has
proposed a number of ways
in which the building works
can be used in the
curriculum including:
measurement and quantities
in maths; engineering work
and construction materials
in science; newsletters in
English; older pupils having
work experience on site;
health and safety; and site
workers becoming mentors
to older pupils. Kingsdale is
a Movement for Innovation
demonstration project.**

Consultation and feedback should continue
through the construction period. Newsletters,
websites and displays can all be used to update
local users, clients and other interested groups
on progress. Where work is taking place at an
existing school, finding ways of linking the
project to the curriculum can benefit pupils
and encourage a positive attitude to the work
taking place.

NEW NORTH LAMBETH SCHOOL, LAMBETH, LONDON
Helping users and clients to envisage the building can help refine the brief.

SHREWSBURY SCHOOL, SHREWSBURY, SHROPSHIRE
With an activities-based brief designers are given a freer range to consider a variety of innovative solutions.

3.3 BRIEF OR OUTPUT SPECIFICATION

A good brief is essential to ensure that the objectives and aspirations of the school and its community are turned to reality when the building work is completed, and it will go a long way towards ensuring a good quality design. A realistic period for the development of the brief, that allows full discussion, is therefore vital.

All potential users must be consulted when developing the brief (see Section 3.2) but the immediate needs of current users should be balanced with a wider view of the school's needs as users change over time. For new schools, it can be more difficult to develop the brief in a participatory way because there will not be any pupils nor will all the staff have been appointed. In this case, the brief needs to be sufficiently flexible to accommodate changing demands.

People often find it hard to envisage what they want in building terms until they have seen it. It is therefore important for users and designers to talk early on so that the designers can use their skills to interpret users' accommodation needs.

To help communicate requirements clearly it is worthwhile involving designers at the briefing stage rather than after the brief has been settled. It is also worthwhile going on joint visits to existing relevant projects. Examples of good aspects of other school buildings can then be built into the brief and aspects that the users dislike can be pointed out to the designers.

The exact nature of a brief depends on the scale of the project and the method of procurement. An activities-based brief allows designers more freedom to propose innovative solutions, but this will only work if time is allowed for discussion between all interested parties to ensure a satisfactory outcome. A detailed room schedule will leave less room for misunderstanding, but will make it more difficult to propose alternative solutions, and this may reduce the chances of high quality design.

A curriculum analysis (see Building Bulletin 82) is a useful way of determining the number of teaching spaces required. It is also important to decide on the other key design priorities at this stage. For example, if a highly sustainable or flexible design is needed then it should be specified clearly.

It is particularly important to be clear about priorities for Private Finance Initiative (PFI) projects where there may be less direct consultation between the users and the design team at the early stage. Experience of this type of project procurement tends to show that the process runs most smoothly when user requirements have been carefully thought through and expressed in the output specification. These requirements should not stifle innovation, but must cover any aspects about which users feel strongly in order to avoid time wasted in producing unacceptable solutions. It is essential to build time into the programme for users to discuss the proposals before they progress too far.

BRIDGE PRIMARY SCHOOL, BANBRIDGE, COUNTY DOWN
It is important to determine the number and scale of spaces needed, taking account of school and community use and also considering possible future change.

3.4 FEASIBILITY STUDIES AND OPTIONS APPRAISALS

Once the need has been established, the school should, for all but the most straightforward projects, work up feasibility studies and consider the costs and benefits of alternative solutions.

For existing schools, the starting point for these should be, firstly, the building development plan, which identifies the longer term building implications of the school's educational plan. This plan is particularly important now that schools have more opportunity to do small-scale capital projects through devolved funding. Secondly, account should be taken of the accommodation assessments carried out as part of the development of the LEA's Asset Management Plan. These will identify shortcomings in terms of the condition of building elements and the sufficiency and suitability of accommodation.

The feasibility study, which should be carried out by LEA officers or a consultant, should look at both immediate and future needs of the school. Many (especially large secondary) schools, which have had a number of additions and alterations over the years, have become 'messy' and a careful plan of rationalisation can improve the situation a great deal. It is unlikely that all work can be carried out at once, but it is easier to do pockets of work within an agreed plan. This is more likely to result in long-term value for money.

The feasibility study should look at all the options and appraise them properly. This will

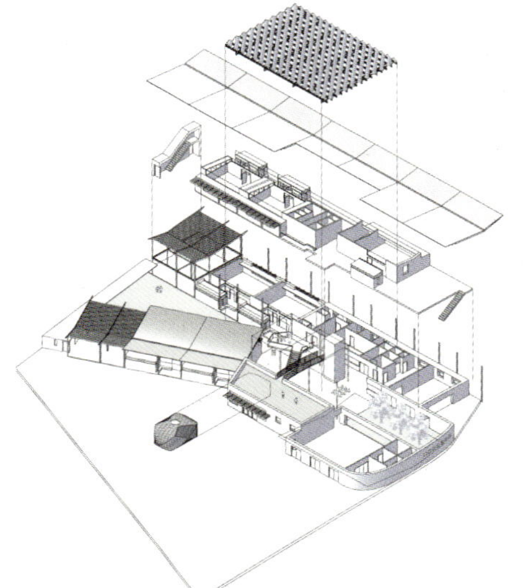

ENTRY FOR RIBA SUSTAINABLITY SCHOOLS COMPETITION
Designs should be based on lifetime costs not just the initial capital cost.

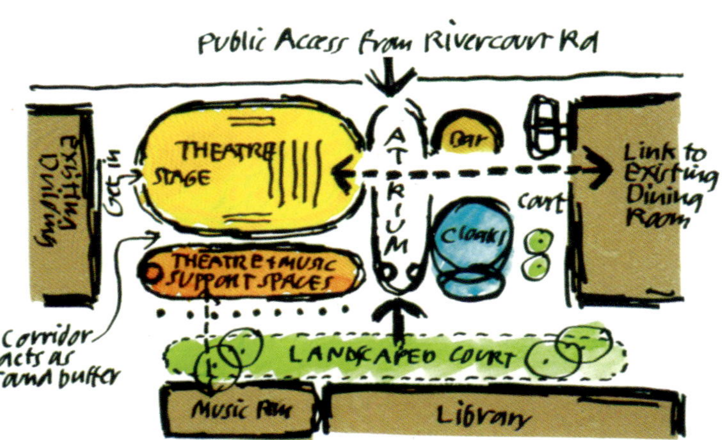

LATYMER UPPER SCHOOL ARTS CENTRE AND THEATRE, HAMMERSMITH, LONDON
Option appraisal means considering all possible levels of changes, from minimal intervention to bigger plans.

TYPICAL SECONDARY SCHOOL PROJECT
Some of the options explored as part of an appraisal looking at major school reorganisation.

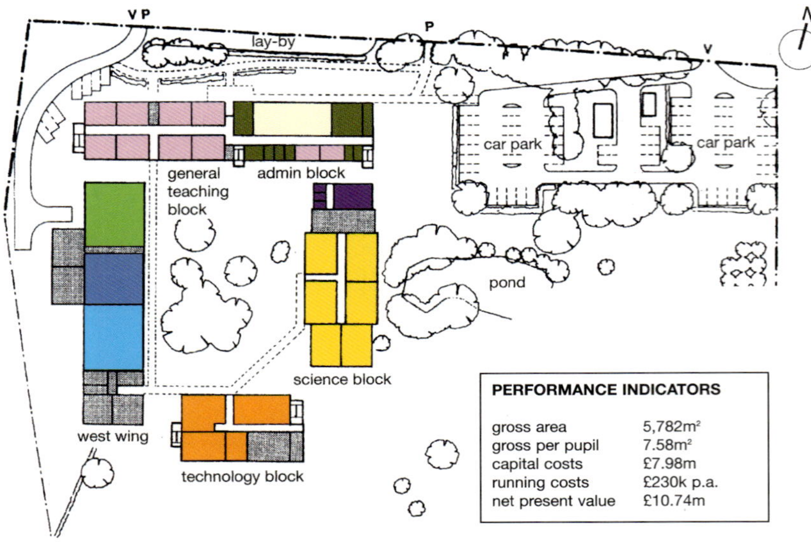

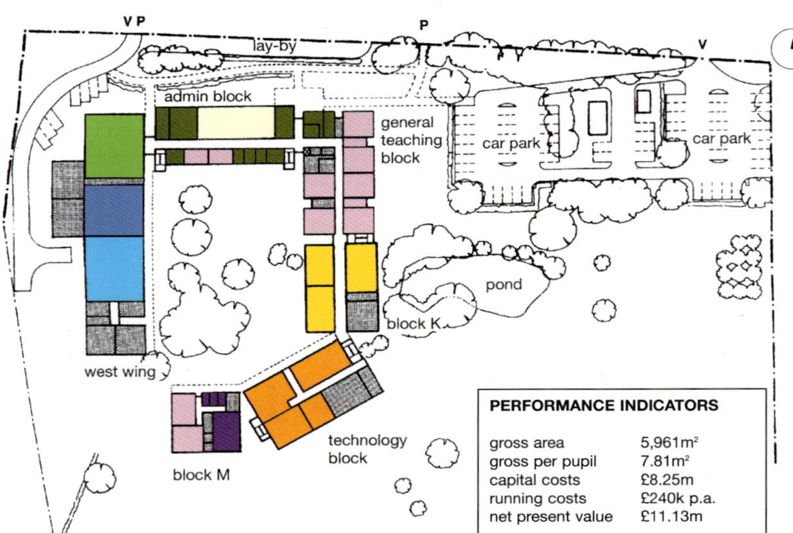

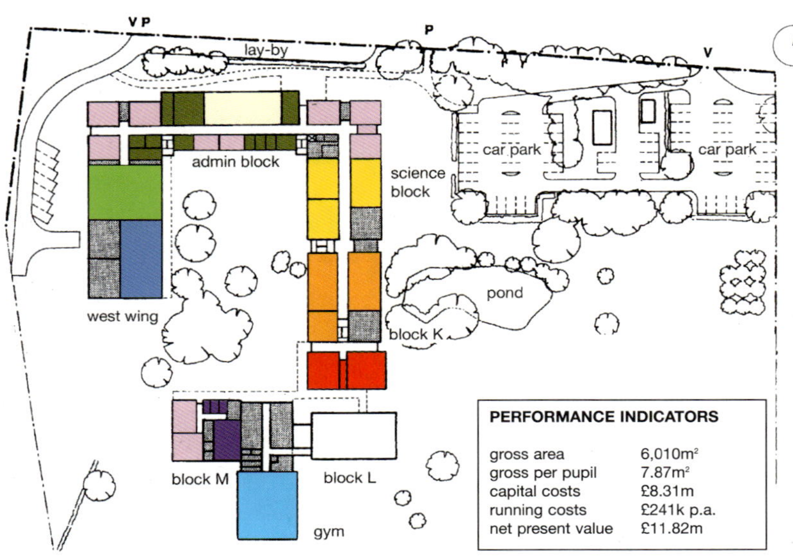

usually involve considering 'do nothing', and 'do minimum' options as a basis for comparison. It is important that the option appraisals look at not just the initial capital cost of building, but also the likely lifetime costs, as the maintenance and running costs of a building over its life are far greater than its initial capital cost. Lifetime costs for each option are adjusted using a standard discount rate, currently 6%, and then added together to give the net present value. This process enables costs occurring at different times to be expressed on a common basis. Option appraisal should also cover qualitative aspects, such as the contribution that buildings make towards raising educational standards, providing community facilities, design quality etc. Illustrative examples of appraisals of project options and their costs are shown in the plans of the secondary school (left).

Options appraisal can also be applied to identifying the most appropriate funding routes. Today, school building work can be funded from various sources including:

- Capital funding devolved to the school;
- LEA mainstream capital programme;
- Targeted capital funds;
- Lottery funding;
- PPP/PFI.

The DfES issues annual guidance on how to obtain funding for new capital projects. Schools and the LEA will need to decide which is the best approach.

HM Treasury's Green Book provides guidance on appraisal principles and the DfES will shortly be publishing guidance on option appraisal in relation to school building projects.

3.5 COST PLANNING

Costs of both new school building and refurbishment work are currently rising faster than general inflation. This is due to the present heavy national demand for building work coming up against skill shortages in the building industry, and to the increased complexity of school building and more stringent construction regulations. Schools with a number of community facilities will usually cost more, and LEAs need to bring together funding streams from various sources in a joined-up way to finance such schemes.

A sustainable, good quality building with low maintenance requirements may cost more initially, but this should be more than offset by lower running costs. So it is important that the lifetime cost of the design is considered rather than just the initial capital cost (see Section 3.4).

Once the overall funding available is known, the project budget should be set. This should include all likely costs including:

- Cost of demolition, building and site works;
- Furniture and fittings;
- Professional fees, if appropriate.

The pie chart opposite shows a typical percentage breakdown for a school project. The professional consultant should develop a detailed cost plan, which should be maintained and kept under review throughout the project.

Once the contract figure is agreed, the client should avoid asking for changes to design or the specification, as even small changes can substantially add to the cost of the project owing to the delay and disruption they can cause to the contractor. Although the cost plan should include a contingency sum for unforeseen circumstances, this is not intended to cover changes in the brief or the design.

3.6 BUILDING PROCUREMENT

There are various ways of undertaking building works at schools, but the four main methods are:

- 'Traditional' procurement;
- Design and Build;
- Public Private Partnerships;
- Partnering.

These are described below. A summary of the main pros and cons of each is shown in the table right.

'Traditional' procurement

Traditional procurement is still the most common form of procurement for small and medium size projects. The client, either the LEA or school, will normally commission consultants to prepare designs and specifications for works that are then constructed by a contractor engaged separately. The contractor is likely to engage sub-contractors for actual construction on site. Traditionally, the contractor offering the lowest bid for the work would be awarded the contract. Once the building contract is finished, the consultants and contractor have limited long-term responsibility for the subsequent performance of the building. Disadvantages of this method include: difficulty in utilising at the most appropriate time the full range of skills and experience of those involved; a focus on initial rather than lifetime costs; a potentially adversarial contractual relationship with greater risk of cost and time overruns.

Design and Build

There are many variants on design and build contracts and in many instances initial design work will be undertaken by the client before transfer to the design and build contractor. Thereafter the contractor takes single-point responsibility for the design and construction. The contractor usually employs consultants for the design element and sub-contractors for the actual construction work. This form of procurement has particular application to fairly simple or standardised buildings, for example, sports halls.

It may be possible for the Design and Build option to be extended to cover maintenance and operation of the facility. This offers the opportunity for adopting innovative solutions that provide greater value for money when considering lifetime costs.

Public Private Partnerships

PPPs are increasingly becoming the main form of procurement for large projects in the schools sector. With PPP, one contractor provides and operates the assets over an extended period, usually 25-30 years. PPP is still a relatively new form of procurement and its application is developing rapidly. PPP at present typically involves the client specifying outputs as opposed to inputs. The benefits of PPP solutions include: greater risk transfer to the private sector partner; use of private sector management to reduce costs; more innovative solutions that offer the possibility of higher quality provision, wider social benefits from more ambitious schemes, and commercial utilisation that can cross-subsidise the project.

PPP procurement is more complex than traditional methods and therefore is less well suited to small building contracts under about £10 million in value. However, a number of smaller projects within a single LEA can be

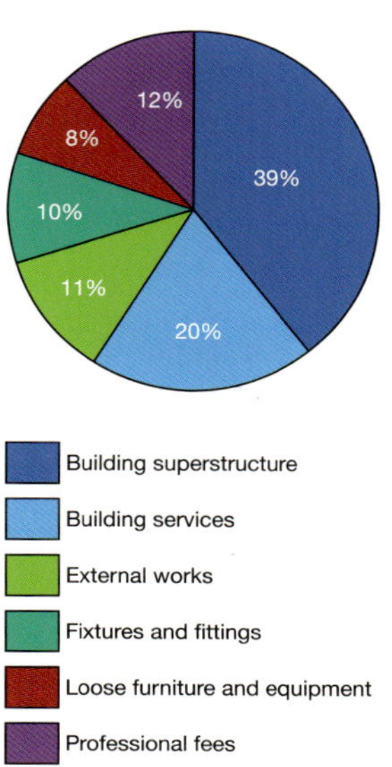

FORMS OF PROCUREMENT: PROS AND CONS				
Client's requirements	Traditional	Design & Build	PPP	Partnering
Time: Fast project completion		Yes		
Cost: Cost needs to be firmly fixed before committing to construct	Yes	Yes	Yes	No
Design: Client requires close involvement with design development		No	No	Yes
Flexibility: Client unable to decide all requirements prior to construction		No	No	Yes
Risk: Client wishes to pass maximum risk to contractor	No	Yes	Yes	
Involvement: Client not able/willing to be closely involved in project	Yes	Yes		No

Yes: Approach more suitable than others

No: Approach not normally appropriate

Note: This table gives a broad indication only, the actual choice will depend on project-specific circumstances

Different methods of procurement are suitable for different contract sizes.

LILLIPUT NURSERY, ST ALBANS, ESSEX
The Lilliput Nursery system is built up from a series of modular units that are manufactured off site. A nursery can be erected in a few days with minimal site disturbance. Advantages include speed, reductions in disruption and mess, and a lower cost. Disadvantages include standardisation and a limited choice of designs.

rolled into a single contract to make this method more feasible. CABE (the Commission for Architecture and the Built Environment) has developed guidance which will be of value to clients entering this procurement route.

Partnering

Arising out of the Rethinking Construction initiative, this approach seeks to address the shortcomings of the traditional procurement route. The benefits of partnering include: integrating the design and construction parties and encouraging the formation of a team that stays together over an entire programme of building works; less confrontational working arrangements; a focus on quality and lowest lifetime costs, not lowest initial costs; more innovative approaches; and continuing improvement over time backed up by performance targets.

The longer-term commitments explicit in this form of procurement make it more appropriate for LEAs with an ongoing programme of building work, rather than for single, one-off, projects.

3.7 PROGRAMMING

The overall programme for the project should be considered at an early stage. Completion dates may be governed by the need to have the accommodation ready to use by a certain date or to spend the grant in a fixed period. To achieve completion on time, good lines of communication need to be established between the design team, contractor and the school.

Programming work is a particular issue in existing school buildings where building work can be disruptive and dangerous. Attempts are often made to maximise the amount of work that can take place out of school hours, particularly over the school holiday periods. This will be more difficult to do if schools extend their daily opening hours and/or are open all the year round to the community.

Methods of construction will be considered as part of the programming stage. For example, prefabrication may be considered as an option for some construction elements, such as external cladding units. This can be particularly useful in a building project at an existing school because it can yield benefits in terms of savings in time, reduced disruption and a cleaner site.

CHRISTCHURCH JUNIOR SCHOOL, DORSET
This replacement and enlargement school project is a Movement for Innovation project. A partnering/framework agreement was used and the project embodies key partnering features. The end users are integrated into the project team, providing continuous feedback in order to improve quality and to maximise opportunities to use the project as an educational tool. The skills of the contractor, sub-contractor and suppliers are maximised by involving them at an early stage to achieve lowest lifetime costs. The contractor and consultants share offices, e-mail, web pages and a single project filing system to allow them to work more closely together. Sub-contractors and suppliers benefit in the same way as the main contractor by way of incentivisations and involvement in value engineering and facilitated workshops. Workmanship and guarantees are negotiated with the whole team.

CHAFFORD HUNDRED LEARNING CAMPUS, ESSEX
Building a new school can be easier to programme than work at an existing school where construction has to be planned to minimise disruption.

KINGSDALE SCHOOL, SOUTHWARK, LONDON
Kingsdale School has set down a series of performance indicators to assess the effect of the forthcoming building project on the educational performance and morale of the school. These are divided into 'quantitative' measures such as 'number of detentions per term' and qualitative indicators such as answers to the question 'do you feel a valued member of the school?' The data will be collected by the school for at least two years after building work is completed.

Prefabricated units are often used for accommodating short-term peaks in pupil numbers, or for relocation purposes during building work on existing sites. These units are quick to erect and can be re-located to other sites, but they must be considered in their truest sense as temporary solutions.

The overall programme for the project should allow sufficient time for fitting out the building prior to it coming into use. As well as setting out loose furniture and equipment, and organising the teaching resources, staff will want to familiarise themselves with the building, including the use of fire and security systems.

3.8 EVALUATION

Once the building has been handed over and is in use, it is good practice to obtain feedback from the users on how the completed building is performing.

Post-project evaluation is an important task which can provide valuable lessons for the future, but it is often forgotten. The process may be carried out on project completion and 12 months or even 24 months afterwards. It involves re-evaluation of the brief and an assessment of the extent to which the thoughts and objectives of the project have been met. Post project evaluation should take place on all school projects and involve all parties – from designers and contractors to school and community users. Evaluation should be based on the following criteria:
- Achievement of the objectives of the brief;
- Achievement of the functionality and content of the scheme;
- Contribution towards educational delivery;
- Spatial satisfaction and flexibility of the accommodation.

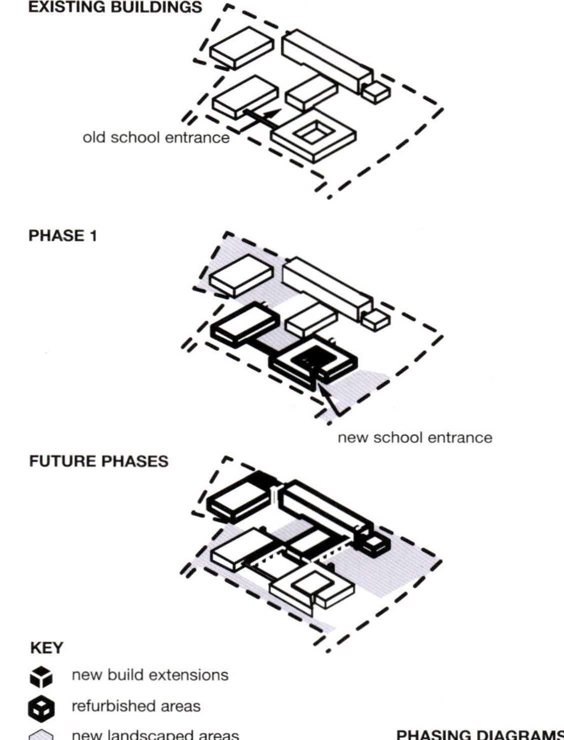

CHARTER HOUSE SCHOOL, SOUTHWARK, LONDON
This refurbishment was planned in a number of phases.

MEADOWSIDE SCHOOL, GLOUCESTERSHIRE
The project continues to educate the pupils even when complete. The special features of the building are explained to the children through labels on pieces of equipment and a paper hand-out. Part of a wall in the entrance hall is exposed to show its construction and services are visible and labelled. Heating controls are also clearly visible.

APPENDIX

A

These three checklists draw together key points that are scattered across a number of sections in the document. Checklist 1 looks at the impact of community use on design of schools, checklist 2 at the impact of inclusion, while checklist 3 summarises security requirements.

Left to right: Stephen Hawking Special Educational Needs School; Gainsborough Adventure Playground, photograph by Martine Hamilton Knight; Alfred Salter School, photograph by Peter Mackertich; Nightingale Nursery, photograph by Graham Turner/Guardian.

CHECKLIST 1:
ACCOMMODATION IMPLICATIONS OF COMMUNITY USE

The increasing use of schools by the wider community is likely to result, over time, in schools having a higher overall floor area. There is also likely to be some change in the balance of spaces. Key points to consider when designing for community use are listed below (see also the publication Raising Standards, Opening Doors).

- Schools should be welcoming and accessible but secure. The extent to which the wider community will have access should be considered at the planning stage (see also under Checklist 3: Security, right).
- The ability to separate areas shared with the community from other school spaces can be useful. It may be appropriate to have a separate entrance for community facilities.
- Many spaces will be designed or adapted for dual use. However there are likely to be some spaces specifically for community use.

- There should if possible be access to a refreshment facility whether this is a cafeteria shared with pupils or a separate small café. Extended opening hours should be considered.
- Additional toilet and changing facilities may be needed.
- Some spaces may need an enhanced specification (e.g. a sports hall to suit competition standards).
- The fact that the school is likely to be open longer hours may mean cleaning and maintenance regimes need to be rethought.

CHECKLIST 2:
ACCOMMODATION IMPLICATIONS OF GREATER INCLUSION

The special needs of all users should be considered throughout the design process from site planning to decisions on services and furniture. Pupils with special needs require assistance from a number of people including teachers and health and social care professionals whose needs must also be considered.

The following facilities are likely to be needed. In many cases these spaces can have dual function.

- Specialist support spaces such as therapy rooms, toilets or hygiene suites.
- Small learning spaces for support teaching or quiet time.
- Access to office space for peripatetic professionals.
- Space for parents and carers to meet, and get support from, staff.
- Storage space for educational and mobility equipment.

The following design points also need to be borne in mind.

- Internal and external space should be accessible to all including those with physical disabilities.
- There should be sufficient movement space for those with physical disabilities in all areas.
- Room temperatures should (as far as practicable) suit all users.
- Colour, light and scents can be used to beneficial effect in learning.
- Lighting and acoustic environment should take account of the hearing impaired.
- Clear circulation routes, colour and texture can help the visually impaired.
- A flexible design allows for changing needs.

CHECKLIST 3:
SECURITY

Security may be more of an issue with more freedom of movement and the school open longer. On the other hand, the school should be a welcoming community centre. Some of the key points are below.

- A site with neighbouring buildings has the advantage of informal visual supervision.
- Well used public routes through the site can also help supervision.
- All boundaries should be clear and the most vulnerable areas made secure.
- Avoid hidden recesses in the building shape.
- Avoid easily accessible roofs.
- Limit points of entry to the school buildings.
- One building is easier to secure than several.
- Entrances should be secure and visible to staff, possibly with a secure lobby.
- Well positioned CCTV cameras help act as a deterent and allow supervision.
- External lighting is important for safety as well as security, particularly as schools will be open longer hours.
- Alarm systems and sprinkler systems should be up to date and well maintained.

B

Left to right: Forest Gate City Learning Centre, Newham, London; Forest Gate City Learning Centre, Newham, London; Montgomery Combined School, Exeter, photograph by Tim Arnold; Park Grove Primary School, York.

ICT INFRASTRUCTURE

ICT is now an essential part of the school environment, used for both educational and administrative purposes. The latest appropriate technological support is needed for all pupils including ports around the school for connection to the school's network, the internet, multi-media libraries, etc. Pupils with SEN may additionally require wireless/ induction loop aids. It is important that the right infrastructure is provided.

Network installations

Networking is now commonplace, allowing greater flexibility with the ability to use any machine, better management and wider access to shared resources. Wireless systems are developing rapidly, in many cases providing an affordable alternative to cabled networks.

It is important to consider carefully a school's needs before making final decisions. This will include looking at the overall installation cost, compatibility with any existing system and curriculum requirements. In many cases a combination of cabled and wireless connections may offer the most flexible solution. Whichever system is chosen it is vital to fully investigate the alternatives and seek expert help with installation.

Wireless

In a wireless network a group of portable computers (usually laptops) are connected to the network by means of radio receiver cards in the PCs which receive data from radio transmitter access points suitably spaced around the school. A single node would typically serve twelve secondary school users simultaneously, depending on users' activity.

Wireless systems can be used with high specification laptops (that do most of the processing rather than relying on a server). An alternative approach being trialled in some schools uses thin client laptops with a higher specification server to process the data centrally. A fat client network, as is often used, is more difficult to upgrade than a thin client network as every laptop has to be upgraded rather than simply upgrading the network software on the server. However, this also depends on the configuration. The newer Windows 2000 supports thin client networking and could lead to more widespread adoption of this type of network. The costs of the laptops is lower in a thin client network. Advantages of a wireless network include:

- Flexibility: computers can be used anywhere within range of the node;
- Ease (and speed) of installation: useful where cabling is difficult or expensive;
- Clean appearance: no visible trunking and less need for suspended ceilings and raised floors.

The main disadvantages of wireless networks are:

- Low data rate: maximum of 11Mbps compares to 100 Mbps to computers on cable network. This is particularly affected by numbers of concurrent users and the type of application. It is far less suitable for multi-media applications. In reality, the throughput may be nearer 6 Mbps due to protocol and security overheads.
- Interference: wireless networks can be prone to interference from other electronic equipment and other radio

networks, especially if poorly installed.

- More difficulty to upgrade: the newer 54Mbps wireless system due out soon will not be compatible with the existing 11Mbps system.
- Battery life: fat client laptops have a typical battery life of two hours. Thin client devices (palmtops, sub notebooks or electronic tablets) can have battery lives of between five and eight hours.

Example applications
1700-place secondary school

The school is on a sprawling campus. It has a cabled network but the addition of a local wireless network allows it to bring computers to classrooms (where teaching resources are available) rather than going to a dedicated IT room. The school is piloting the network in the modern foreign languages department with 16 laptops in a serviced trolley, and a printer on top. This is stored in the local office to be used in any classroom in the department. If the pilot proves successful the plan is to have a similar trolley in every department. The school is finding the system very useful as a supplement to fixed, cabled PCs which can handle faster data transfers.

210-place primary school

This is a primary with typical accommodation: a Victorian main building, a timber framed annex, two mobile classrooms. A wireless radio network has been installed with three transmitters (able to reach the mobile classrooms with a booster aerial at low cost). 16 laptops are kept in a purpose-built cupboard in the school office (wired up for re-charging) and taken to classrooms as needed. Infants work on laptops in groups of five or six, each sharing three laptops, juniors share

them between the whole class. The school finds the arrangement adequate and doesn't feel the need for a dedicated IT room.

Installation

Radio access points have a range of about 30m in a school building but this can vary up to 200m in open space so it is essential to do a site survey. Metal in the building structure, including reinforcing in concrete walls and floors and metal barriers such as permanent metal formwork or foil-faced plasterboard can cause problems. Radio can, however, penetrate a metal stud plasterboard partition that is not foil faced. Reception can be improved by (inexpensive) antennae.

Cabling will still be needed to link access points/base stations and main servers which will all need power. As portable computers rely on batteries it is important to provide the facility to recharge the machines. Purpose-designed cupboards or trolleys (which will need their own storage space) are available.

Wireless connections can also be made over long distances such as between schools using directional antennae, microwave and laser links.

It is especially important to have a wireless network configured by specialists as this can affect system security (for example from hackers) and performance.

BECTA Technology Briefing Paper Wireless Local Area Networks (WLANs)' - available at www.naace.org - provides useful guidance and contains a number of references including on standards and health and safety.

Cabling

Cabling is likely to be needed to some extent in all installations, particularly for a

large number of users and where a number of multi-media applications are used. The current standard of cabling for connection to devices is untwisted pair cable (UTP) category 5E. Backbone cables between servers and main switches are more likely to be in optic fibre (UTP has a maximum length of 90m). In this way a high data rate can be provided on the backbone, currently around 1GBps but likely to increase to 10GBps in future. There are guidelines on installation of network cables such as ANSI/TIA/EIA-568B, CENELEC 11801 and CENELEC-EN 50173/4. As cable types may need to be upgraded in the future, sufficient space in main trunking routes should be allowed to accommodate future needs.

Guarantees on system installation are essential. The main testing standards for copper is the permanent link test (TIA-TSB-95 and ISO/IEC-11801-2000). Appropriate testing devices (such as Fluke or Wirescope) should be used.

Infrastructure

As technology is constantly changing, building infrastructure should be designed for change. It is important to consider, for example, trunking routes and the positioning and servicing of servers. The relevant standard for this is 'Pathways and Spaces' (ANSI/TIA/EIA-569-A).

If file servers are sited in unoccupied rooms the need for air conditioning may be reduced as the computers themselves can withstand higher temperatures than people. However there have been reports of unreliability where several servers are located in a small space without ventilation. Access will be required for management on a regular basis and a secure ICT office is a preferred solution.

REFERENCES

PUBLICATIONS

GENERAL DESIGN

Area Guidelines for Schools. DfEE Building Bulletin 82. HMSO (1996). ISBN 0 11 270921 4 (revised version available in 2002).

Designing for 3-4 Year Olds. DfEE (1999). ISBN 0 85522 986 1. *

Assessing the Net Capacity of Schools (guidance document). DfES (2001). DfES/0739/2009. *

City Learning Centres (Design Guide). DfEE (revised 2000). *

Designs for Learning: 55 Exemplary Educational Facilities. PEB, OECD (2001).

SPECIALIST SPACES

Science Accommodation in Secondary Schools: A Design Guide. DfEE Building Bulletin 80. The Stationery Office (Second Edition 1999). ISBN 0 11 271039 5.

Design and Technology Accommodation in Secondary Schools: A Design Guide. DfEE Building Bulletin 81. HMSO (1996). ISBN 0 11 270917 6.

Music Accommodation in Secondary Schools. DfEE Building Bulletin 86. The Stationery Office (1997). ISBN 0 11 271002 6.

Art Accommodation in Secondary Schools. DfEE Building Bulletin 89. The Stationery Office (1998). ISBN 0 11 271029 8.

Modern Foreign Languages Accommodation: A Design Guide. DfEE Building Bulletin 92. The Stationery Office (2000). ISBN 0 11 271093 X.

Designing Space for Sports and Arts. DfEE (2000).*

Sport England Guides (e.g. Sports Halls: Design). Sport England Publications.

INCLUSION & COMMUNITY USE

Designing for Pupils with Special Educational Needs: Special Schools. DfES Building Bulletin 77. The Stationery Office (Revised 1997). ISBN 0 11 270796 3.

Access for Disabled People to School Buildings: Management and Design Guide. DfEE Building Bulletin 91. The Stationery Office (1999). ISBN 0 11 271062 X.

Inclusive School Design. DfEE Building Bulletin 94. The Stationery Office (2001). ISBN 0 11 271109 X.

Raising Standards, Opening Doors. DfEE (1999). ISBN 0 855224473 8. *

LANDSCAPE/EXTERNAL DESIGN

The Outdoor Classroom – 2nd Edition. DfEE Building Bulletin 71. The Stationery Office (1999). ISBN 0 11 271061 1.

Car Park and Landscape Design (Sport England Guidance Note). ISBN 1 86078 101 2 (Ref 886).

ENVIRONMENTAL DESIGN & SERVICES

Schools' Environmental Assessment Method (SEAM). DfEE Building Bulletin 83. The Stationery Office (1996). ISBN 0 11 270920 6.

Guidelines for Environmental Design in Schools. DfEE Building Bulletin 87. The Stationery Office (1997). ISBN 0 11 27013 1.

Lighting Design for Schools. DfEE Building Bulletin 90. The Stationery Office (1999). ISBN 0 11 271041 7.

Natural Ventilation in Non-domestic Buildings. CIBSE Application Manual, AM10 (1997). Chartered Institution of Building Services Engineers.

Wireless Local Area Networks (WLANs). Becta (2001).

ORGANISATIONS

Arts Council of England
14 Great Peter Street
London SW1P 3NQ
T: 020 7973 6517
E: enquiries@artscouncil.org.uk
www.artscouncil.org.uk

Association of Noise Consultants
6 Trap Road
Guilden Morden
Royston
Herts SG8 0JE
T: 01763 852958
www.association-of-noise-consultants.co.uk

British Educational Communications and Technology Agency (Becta)
Milburn Hill Road
Science Park
Coventry CV4 7JJ
T: 024 7641 6994
F: 024 7641 1418
E: becta@becta.org.uk

British Research Establishment (BRE) Schools
E: Dickinsonm@bre.co.uk

Chartered Institution of Building Services Engineers (CIBSE)
Delta House
222 Balham High Road
London SW12 9BS
T: 020 8675 5211
www.cibse.org

Commission for Architecture in the Built Environment (CABE)
The Tower Building
11 York Road
London SE1 7NX
T: 020 7960 2400
F: 020 7960 2444
E: enquiries@cabe.org.uk
www.cabe.org.uk

Department for Culture, Media and Sport (DCMS)
2-4 Cockspur Street
London SW1Y 5DH
T: 020 7211 6200
www.culture.gov.uk

Department for Education and Skills
Sanctuary Buildings
Great Smith Street
London SW1P 3BT
T: 020 7925 5000
www.dfes.gov.uk for general information from the DfES or www.teachernet.gov.uk/school buildings for specific information related to school building design

Furniture Industry Research Association (FIRA)
Maxwell Road
Stevenage
Hertfordshire SG1 2EW
T: 01438 777700
F: 01438 777800
www.fira.co.uk

Health and Safety Executive
Rose Court
2 Southwark Bridge
London SE1 9HS
T: 0870 1545500
E: hseinformationservices@natbrit.com
www.hse.gov.uk

Home Office
7th floor
50, Queen Anne's Gate
London SW1H 9AT
T: 0870 0001585
E: public.enquiries@homeoffice.gsi.gov.uk
www.homeoffice.gov.uk
Website includes useful information on fire precautions and fire safety

Institute of Structural Engineers
11 Upper Belgrave Street
London SW1X 8BH
T: 020 7235 4535
www.istructe.org.uk

Learning through Landscapes
3rd Floor, Southside Offices
The Law Courts
Winchester SO23 9DL
T: 01962 846 258
F: 01962 869 099
www.ltl.org.uk

HEALTH & SAFETY

*Improving Security in Schools
(Managing School Facilities Guide 4).*
DfEE. The Stationery Office (1996).
ISBN 0 11 270916 8.

*Fire Safety (Managing School
Facilities Guide 6).* DfEE. The
Stationery Office (2000).
ISBN 0 11 271040 9.

*Furniture and Equipment in Schools:
a Purchasing Guide (Managing
School Facilities Guide 7).* DfEE
The Stationery Office (2000).
ISBN 0 11 271092 1.

THE BUILDING PROCESS

Asset Management Plan guides
DfEE (2001)*
AMP Guide 1: Framework
AMP Guide 3: Condition Assessment
AMP Guide 4: Suitability Assessment
AMP Guide 5: Sufficiency Assessment

*Appraisal and Evaluation in Central
Government.* HM Treasury (1997).

*A Guide for School Governors:
Developing School Buildings.* RIBA
(2000).

*Achieving Quality in Local Authority
PFI Building Projects,* Public Private
Partnerships Programme (2001).

POLICY PAPERS AND
REGULATIONS ETC

*The Education (School Premises)
Regulations 1999. Statutory
Instrument 1999 No 2.* (1999) The
Stationery Office.

Achieving Success (DfEE White
Paper 2001).

Better Public Buildings. dcms (2000).

Rethinking Construction – Sir John
Egan's Report (1998).

*A Better Quality of Life – a Strategy for
Sustainable Development for the UK,*
DETR (1999). The Stationery Office.

*Achieving a Better Quality of Life –
Review of Progress towards
Sustainable Development,*
Government annual report 2000.
DETR, The Stationery Office (2000).

Full Day Care. National Standards.
DfES (2001) Circular
DfES/0488/2001.
ISBN 1 84185 516 2. *

*Sessional Day Care, National
Standards.* DfES (2001) Circular*

Crèches. National Standards. DfES
(2001) Circular*

*Excellence for all children, Meeting
Special Educational Needs* (DfEE
Green Paper). HMSO (1997).
ISBN 0 10 137852 1.

*The Special Educational Needs and
Disability Act* (2001).

School I'd Like. The Guardian (5 June
2001).

FORTHCOMING
PUBLICATIONS FROM DfES

Schools Building and Design Unit is
producing design guides on the
following in the near future.
Acoustic Design for Schools. DfES
Building Bulletin 93. March 2002.

Security.

Sports and Performing Arts Spaces.

City Academies.

*Estates Management (a Guide for
School Governors).*

*DfES circulars and AMP guidance
documents are available from:
Department for Education and Skills
Publications Centre
PO Box 5050
Sherwood Park
Annesley
Nottingham NG15 0DJ
T: 0845 602 2260
F: 0845 603 3360
E: dfes@prologistics.co.uk

Local Government Task Force
108-110 Judd Street
London WC1H 9PX
T: 020 7837 8286
F: 020 7813 3060
E: info@lgtf.org.uk
www.lgtf.org.uk

Movement for Innovation (M4I)
Building 9
BRE
Bucknalls Lane
Garston
Watford WD25 9XX
T: 01923 664820
F: 01923 664822
www.m4i.org.uk

**National Association of Advisers
for Computers in Education
(NAACE)**
PO Box 6511
Nottingham NG11 8TN
T: 0870 240 0480
F: 0870 241 4115
E: carolyn@naace.org

New Opportunities Fund (NOF)
Heron House
322 High Holborn
London WC1V 7PW
T: 0845 000 0120
www.nof.org.uk

OECD
2, rue André Pascal
F-75775 Paris Cedex 16
France
T: +33 1.45.24.82.00
www.oecd.org

**Royal Institute of British
Architects (RIBA)**
66 Portland Place
London W1A 4AD
T: 020 7580 5533
www.architecture.com
Website includes a national list of
architectural practices and their
specialisms

**Royal Institution of Chartered
Surveyors (RICS)**
12 Great George Street
Parliament Square

London SW1P 3AD
T: 020 7222 7000
www.rics.org.uk

School Works
The Mezzanine-South
Elizabeth House
39 York Road
London SE1 7NQ
T: 020 7401 5333
E: Mail@school-works.org

**Special Educational Needs Joint
Initiative for Training (SeNJIT)**
University of London Institute of
Education
20 Bedford Way
London WC1 0AL
T: 020 7612 6273
F: 020 7612 6994
www.ioe.ac.uk/teepnnp/SENJIT

Solar Century
91-94 Lower Marsh
London SE1 7AB
T: 020 7803 0100
F: 020 7803 0101
www.solarcentury.co.uk

Sport England
16 Upper Woburn Place
London WC1H 0QP
T: 020 7273 1500
www.english.sports.gov.uk

Ultralab
Anglia Polytechnic University
Central Campus
Victoria Road South
Chelmsford
Essex CM1 1LL
T: 01245 252 009
F: 01245 252 047
E: enquiries@ultralab.anglia.ac.uk
www.ultralab.anglia.ac.uk

Watermark
OGC Buying.Solutions
Royal Liver Building
Pier Head
Liverpool
L3 1PE
T: 0151 227 4262
F: 0151 224 2353
E: watermark@ogcbs.gov.uk
www.watermark.gov.uk

CASE STUDY ACKNOWLEDGEMENTS

SCHOOL	DESIGNERS
ACE Centre	WS Atkins - Oxford
Alfred Salter Primary School	Southwark Building Design Service
Bexley Neighbourhood Nursery	Birds Portchmouth Russum Architects
Barnhill School	Terence O'Rourke
Blenheim High School	Grasby O'Neill with A&B Branch (DfEE)
Bridge Primary School	Samuel Stevenson and Sons
British Airways Waterside (offices)	Niels Torp
Burton Borough Studios, Burton Borough School	McMorran and Gatehouse Architects
Caterhatch Infant School extension	Stephen Davy Peter Smith Architects
Chafford Hundred Learning Campus	Nicholas Hare Architects
Charter School refurbishment	Penoyre and Prasad Architects
Childsplay Nursery	Hampshire County Architects
Chudleigh Primary School	Devon County Council Property Department
Cleveden Secondary	HLM Architects
Colfox School	Terence O'Rourke
Coram Family	Monahan Blythen Architects
Cromwell Park Primary School	Cambridgeshire County Architects
Cyril Jackson Primary School	Bob Byron Architects
Debden Park High School	ACP
Dixons City Technology College	John Brunton Partnership
Djanogly City Technology College	Architects and Building Branch, DES
Douay Martyrs School	Grieg and Stephenson
Fairly House School	Jestico and Whiles
Firth Park Community College	Sheffield Design and Property
Forest Gate City Learning Centre	Building Design Division, London Borough of Newham
Frensham Heights School	Burrell Foley Fischer
Gainsborough Adventure Playground	Groundworks Architects
Glastonbury Thorn Primary School	Buckinghamshire County Architects
Great Binfield Primary School	Hampshire County Architects
Haslemere First School	Todd Architects and Planners
Haute Vallee School	architecture plb
Haverstock School	Fielden Clegg Bradley Architects
Hayes School	PCKO
Heinavaara Elementary School	Cuningham Group
Jersey College for Girls	architecture plb
Jews Free School	Terence O'Rourke
King Alfred School	van Heyningen and Haward Architects
Kingsdale School	dRMM
Kingsmead Primary School. Entry into RIBA sustainable schools competition	Sir Colin Stansfield Smith and John Pardey
Kingswood Primary School. Entry into RIBA sustainable schools competition	Baker-Brown McKay Architects
Knightwood Primary School	Hampshire County Architects
Latymer Upper School Arts Centre and Theatre	van Heyningen and Haward Architects
Lilliput Nursery, St Alban's Catholic Primary School	Cottrell and Vermeulen Architecture
Lund Ladugardsmarke Elementary School	Olaf Meiby

SCHOOL	DESIGNERS
Manorfield Park	Penoyre and Prasad Architects
Meadowside School	Gloucestershire County Council
Merryfield Nursery	Southwark Building Design Service
Millennium Primary School	Edward Cullinan Architects
New North Lambeth	Penoyre and Prasad Architects
Newtown Primary School	Hampshire County Architects
Notley Green Primary	Allford Hall Monaghan Morris
Park Grove Primary School	York Consultancy, City of York Council
Parrs Wood High School	Edmund Kirby Architects
Pen Green EEC	Northamptonshire County Council Property Services
Perthcelyn Community Primary School	Rhondda Cynon Taff Property Consultancy
Pokesdown Primary School	Format Milton Architects
Queen's Inclosure Primary School	Hampshire County Architects
Richard Attenborough Centre for Disability and the Arts	Bennetts Associates
Royal Docks Community School	Building Design Division, London Borough of Newham
Rydal School	Colwyn Foulkes & Partners
Shrewsbury School, music school and auditorium	Pringle Richards Sharratt
Sir George Monoux Sixth Form College	van Heyningen and Haward Architects
South Camden Community School	van Heyningen and Haward Architects
St Alban's Catholic School	Cottrell and Vermeulen Architecture
St Anthony's School	van Heyningen and Haward Architects
St Clare's RC Primary School	Cottrell and Vermeulen Architecture
St George's School	Reiach and Hall Architects
St Mungos, Glasgow	PJMP
St Paul's Church of England Primary School	Partridge Viner Craddock Group
St Vincent's Roman Catholic Primary School	Cottrell and Vermeulen Architecture
Stadtische Gesamtschule Barmen	Parade Architekten
Stephen Hawking Special Educational Needs School	Haverstock Associates
Summerfields Nursery	Stephenson Bell
Swanlea Secondary School	Percy Thomas Architects with Hampshire County Architects
Tanbridge House School	architecture plb
Thomas Telford City Technology College	Barnsley Hewitt and Mallinson
Tulse Hill Primary School	Allford Hall Monaghan Morris
Victoria Infants School	Urban Design Architects' Unit, Sandwell MBC with A&B Branch (DfEE)
Wakefield Grammar School, nursery	HLM Architects
Weobley Primary School	Hereford and Worcester County Council
Westborough Primary School	Cottrell and Vermeulen Architecture
Whiteley Primary	Hampshire Country Architects
Willowtree Primary School	Unicorn Architects Department
Windmill Montessori Nursery School	Sergison Bates Architects with Bennetts Associates
Wonnelly School, CDT block	Southwark Building Design Service
Woodlea Primary School	Hampshire County Council
Yewlands Secondary School, Classroom of the Future	Education Design Group

For contact details of UK architects see www.architecture.com